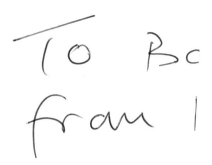

In preparation for the London Marathon, I stopped playing football in February 2017. After completing the marathon – without walking or stopping – my pulled hamstring became torn. Owing to injury, I did not play football again until after the 2018 London Marathon. In this sixteen-month period, I set myself the target of writing a book about football and completing it before I started playing again. In April 2018, I put down my pen and put on my footy trainers. Well not strictly true, as you will see, if you make it to the end of this book.

Ours: Football

Does our game still belong to us?

Lee Ingham

Published in the United Kingdom by:

Ours: Books,
204 Oak Bank,
Shaw Lane,
Leeds LS6 4DH

No rights reserved as football belongs to everyone.
Feel free to share and use.
£1 of each sale will be donated to
the Football Supporters Federation (FSF)

A CIP version of this book is available at the British Library

First printed May 2019
Cover design by Present Works
Illustrations by James Dawson
Published by Ours: Books

ISBN 978-1-5272-4086-5

Dedicated to all those to whom football belongs including one of the most passionate, my Dad.

Also to Chris Slamon, aka Bully, who features in this book and unexpectedly died whilst the book was at the publishers. As Jim Bowen rightly said about our mate:

"You cannot beat a bit of Bully"

Thank you to Peter Lowes, Brett 'can't play for toffee' Jacob, Cockney Keith and Anne Marie 'Guffer' Garnett for reading it. Thanks also to James 'Boiling' Dawson for the drawings, most of which fortuitously contain pictures of Chris Slamon. Thanks also for approval from Aidrian Hirst, Andrew Holt, Bob Ingham (Senior and Junior), Jeff 'BOGOF' Brown and Mike Garlick. Thanks also to all other contributors and those that have made a contribution to the Football Supporters Federation. Together we are stronger. UTC's

Contents

Me, hand delivering a copy of 'Ours:Football'
For some reason there's a glare in the photo

ABOUT ME AND THE BOOK, BY ME

Writing this book has been easy. From the outset it became
apparent that football is in every part of my life. For instance,
when I started writing I noticed that above my bed was a
blown up photo of my mates and me at a game in the 90's[1].
I also noticed that the windows have not been cleaned
despite a bet - with the Leeds supporting 'Gary the Window
Cleaner' - that Chris Woods would score plenty of goals for
Burnley and if he did Gary would clean my windows for free.
At least Woods did his part of the deal. I have also noticed

---

[1] stood up on the Longside for the last time before the ground was
made all seater. Which one is me? Clue : back cover

that when I meet men for the first time, we break the ice by establishing which team we support, then we are off. You will probably have football in most aspects of your life. If so, this book will hold a mirror up to your life. If not, it will hold a mirror up to the life of someone you know.

I am a middle-aged, white, working class male, who likes going to the pub. Nowadays though, I live with middle-class trappings, such as a season ticket for a son who rarely attends. Like you, I watch, talk and support football. Footballing outsiders describe us as 'passionate' about football. We just see football as a part of normal life. However, writing this book has helped me realise how big a part of our normal life it is.

For at least the last sixty years, my Dad, my son and me have watched The Clarets at Turf Moor. More recently (last 15 years) my son and me have driven from Leeds to watch Burnley at Turf Moor; home to Burnley Football Club for 166 years – that's 33 years before the Football League was even founded. My son's first visit to Burnley included a trip to the Park View (pub opposite the ground) where I presented him to the lads. I didn't take him on the game – he was three months old – but Kunta Kinta style, I held him up to the ground and named him 'Bobby Ingham'. He was the fourth consecutive Robert Ingham to watch The Clarets (my middle name is Robert).

This book claims that football clubs belong to 'us' - the supporters. However, in the case of Burnley Football Club, the Inghams can take ownership a step further. It may come as a surprise – it was not to me – but Turf Moor was built on Ingham land i.e. farmland owned by a Burnley resident called 'Ingham'[2]. As I said at the time of finding this out, 'I always knew we were there at the very beginning and that we helped create football!' I just need to ascertain whether this qualifies us to be recipients of the Football Royalties Scheme that I am championing. Details to follow.

This book asks three questions. Firstly, is football ours? To which the answer is yes. Secondly, why are our football clubs being taken away from us? Finally, can we do anything to prevent theft of our clubs? If you manage to read the book to the end, you will see that I also share stories about playing, watching, talking about, singing about and supporting football. To help you make it to the end, I have purposefully kept the stories short. Like me you may not be a big reader but do not worry each chapter is no longer than a reasonable visit to the Little Boys room.

---

[2] Google 'Turf Moor Ingham' and you will see a link to a book called The Lancashire Witchcraft Conspiracy'. In this book (p.212 -213) it states: In the sixteenth century, branches of the Ingham family were located from Whalley through to Colne .. but the main families were located in a small area of Burnley. 'The site of highest status regarding the **Ingham** properties was the farming operation at Fulledge (Burnley), this incorporated **Turf Moor**, now the site of the Burnley Football Club stadium.' BTW – ignore the first bit of page 212 where it inaccurately states that 'Demdike's daughter carried the surname of Ingham at the time of her marriage'. Demdike was one of the Lancashire witches and also the pet name given one of my first girlfriends by Jeff Brown.

INTRODUCTION

In January 2017, in an attempt to keep out of the pub, I decided to try reading books. By mid-March I was pretty chuffed with myself, having read two. Both footy related[3]. I even went to a book-signing for the second book. At this event, I informed the author James Brown - I sort of know him through someone I used to play footy with – that his book will not be as good as the other book I had read that year (Joey Barton's autobiography). On reflection, as well as telling the truth, I was probably trying to score one for Burnley over our former rivals Leeds.

In the midst of this book reading frenzy, I had another idea for keeping out of the pub. Why don't I write my own book about footy? With all due respect (a phrase that normally precedes the opposite), if James Brown can write a book on football, then so can I. Sorry James. Equally, if Lee Ingham can, then I'm sure that you can too.

In April 2017 I completed the London Marathon – without stopping or walking – despite having a significant hamstring

---

[3] James Brown's Above Head Height and Joey Barton's autobiography No Nonsense

injury. My torn hamstring stopped me playing for a further twelve months. When I 'stopped' playing, I decided to write a book about football, and set myself the target of completing a book to coincide with my return to playing.

Not playing for sixteen months was torture. However, as I complete this book on the way to the 2018 London Marathon, I plan not to damage my hamstring tomorrow; so that I can return to playing asap. Obviously, on my return to football, the world will return to its natural resting place i.e. Lee Ingham putting through that killer pass from his deep lying 5–a-side stopper role.

SECTION 1

PLAYING OUR GAME

Me, ghosting past Chris Slamon, Trevor-Stevens-Stylee

I have put this first, because like in any sport, there is no better aspect of football than playing it. When you can no longer play football it must be a sad, sad day. Unfortunately, I am not far away from experiencing it myself.

Chapter 1

My football career

Up until February 2017, for 25 years, I had played 5–a-side at least once a week. In 'Above Head Height', James Brown asserts that many professional footballers stop playing once they stop getting paid. In addition, we all know of 'players' who have even agreed a transfer that will lead to them being unlikely to play. This is anathema to what James calls 'real players'. Not only are real players not paid, but we pay to play and I am not just talking about money. For instance, prior to James signing of his book in Headingley, I organised a game between my current Monday night and former Wednesday night teams. An hour before the game I visited a physio (I used to play 5-a-side with him) for a massage and ultrasound. Owing to a football injury (hamstring) I had not played for five weeks, and in a month's time I would be 'running'[4] the London 2017 Marathon. I know. I shouldn't have been playing.

In the 'warm-up', I used my experience and made sure that everyone knew that I had a hamstring injury. I also made it

---

[4] Whatever happened to jogging? At least I have remained faithful!

clear that I may need to spend quite a lot of time in the goals. Predictably, this assertion had a domino effect on my Wednesday night colleagues. Jeff was the first domino, telling me he also had a hamstring injury. Then Red Roger informed me that he last played football two years ago as part of my 50th celebrations (Lancashire 10 v Pudds 1). Scouse Neil 'just has a knee injury' which would not - according to him - 'stop him banging in a load of goals'. That just left Porno Andrew (last minute stand in), who did not need an injury because he was looking a bit weighty and from memory was also a bit shit.

As the organiser and loudest pre-match whinger, I pulled rank ensuring I started in goal[5]. In the back of my mind, I began to think that the massage and ultrasound seemed to have made a difference. Consequently, I started to plan a cameo performance, where towards the end of the game I would come out of the goal to adopt my low maintenance position of centre half (see end notes) a position I'd become accustomed to over the past fifteen years. In the cameo, I saw myself feeding Scouse Neil with pearler passes. At this stage, it may be useful to explain that in my 5-a-side brain, passes have become the new goals. 'Goals' are for pussies scored by prima donnas with egos that require massaging. In other words, Scouse Neil. Sorry Neil.

---

[5] Normally dead time, allied with risk that you may become the target of ridicule should you let in a sitter.

On reflection, I had probably spent almost a day organising this game. With the 'no- shows'[6] adding to the time spent. In addition, I had spent £34 for a physio and almost a third of the game in the goal. As I submit this analysis to paper, I question whether it was worth it? And the answer is YES.

So why? Well for one reason, playing football is one of the few chances I have to be creative. As evidenced in the game above by my 'Cruyff-turn, back pass to the keeper'[7]. Yes, you read it right. The Cruyff pull back and swivel improvised to make a pass back to the keeper. From a purist's point of view, it's probably wrong to use this thing of beauty in a back pass. Nonetheless, you must admit, it was creative.

The Monday Nighters v Wednesday Nighters game was corpulent with people who also believe that their pass, goal, foul, is their chance to express themselves. That is why, at the age of 52, I used the book signing evening to recruit for a new Thursday Night game. I informed people that the game will be indoors – in honour of hamstring injuries – and that it will be followed by compulsory post match pub attendance. The 'shared belief' also explains why three people signed up on the night. Six people on the day, if you include the guy providing me with the pre-match physio, who said he and a couple of mates would play. James' book

---

[6] including James Brown whose book talks about him loving playing at the location where I had arranged the game.

[7] Copyrighted by Lee Ingham

explains in detail the 'secret' world of 5–a-side and why we 'real footballers' go through what we go through. His book is worth a read. After you've read Joey Barton's book, that is.

You will be glad to hear that there is more about my 'illustrious playing career' further on.

Chapter 2

My Dad playing football

Firstly, let me describe the environment in which my Dad shares this story. We are having tea at his older sister's. She has used a wheeler to transport meals from the kitchen to the big table in 'the room'. The unspoken back story to the meal is the increasing likelihood that these kind of events are becoming less and less likely to happen again. We are all going to die, however both my Auntie Beryl and my Dad (whom I see for the first time trying to hide his shaking hand) are approaching full -time. They may even have sadly moved into extra-time.

After eating, I use the family tree on Auntie Beryl's front room wall to try and unearth stories about my Granddad and further back. I engineer this because Auntie Beryl has stories that may soon be lost, unlike my Dad, whose is information-light when it comes to back-catalogue family stuff. I suspect that he considers the retention of family history to be what he would call 'a girl's game'. Anyway, even if my Dad does know any family history, he isn't going to miss the opportunity to talk about football. Rather than talking about watching football – an area in which he considers himself an expert - he makes a rare sortie into the world of him playing football.

This is his story. I hope I have done it justice. Although it will be less detailed as my Dad is usually 'generous with his time'[8]. Especially when talking about his passion - football.

According to my Dad, there were 100 children at Back Lane Junior School and 'if you had boots you were in the team'. As a small school, Back Lane had one of the weaker football teams. In fact, in three years, Back Lane only won one game. It's in this game that my Dad played a significant part i.e. he scored the only goal.

In the story my Dad explained how against Rosegrove Juniors, the Back Lane keeper thumped the ball away from an army of 'much bigger Rosegrove lads'. Back Lane and the goalkeeper had been under siege. As my Dad fled Mafeking, with the big lads baring down on him, the goalkeepers kick landed near him at which stage he executed the 'biggest toe end I have ever seen'. Miraculously the ball found the bottom corner, beating a keeper who had spent most of the game sitting on his line, with his back against the post. In fact, as my Dad made back Lane's solitary sortie into their half he had been looking out of the back of the goal the other way.

---

[8] Probably the most generous explanation of a person I have ever heard (Debbie Robinson).

At the end of the game, my Dad was carried off the pitch, on the shoulders of his schoolmates. Not a bad story – though my shortened version doesn't do my Dad's achievement justice.

Yet it is the next bit of his story that I will always remember. It is rarer than a Back Lane goal. As my Dad drew his footballing story towards the full-time whistle - most of his stories included extra time and penalties - he described how he had walked back from the game with his shirt wrapped around his shoulders. He then said how he would 'always remember that feeling' as he neared home and crossed Piccadilly Road Bridge, over the trainline where he was sometimes lucky enough to bask in the steam from the passing trains. Then he fell silent. Yes, silent My Dad! Talking about football! It was if he had entered the zone - about to take a penalty - visualising where he was going to place it.

He never told us what he 'remembered' when crossing the bridge with the jumper round his shoulders. He did however go on to tell us how the goal led to him being picked for the West of Burnley Town team and how this was probably the zenith of his footballing career. Understandable, as I am sure you will agree: 'We played up Townley, with a proper ref and in Hargher Cloughs shirts. It was the first time I had ever played with nets. I felt like an international.'

The story probably captures the way that we men work. That even in football – the thing we probably talk the most about – we will not share our feelings. If you are a man reading this, can you remember expressing a feeling about football other than anger, elation, boredom, laughter, pride, crying or despair? If so, you're a better man than me. Although, not much better, as it is a pretty big list.

Chapter 3

Being the reserve

If you are like myself, this form of 'not playing' is guaranteed to raise strong feelings. I am not referring to the type of 'not playing' that I recently experienced in my sixteen-month absence through injury. Instead, I am referring to something I have buried. A type of 'not playing', the unearthing of which could open old wounds but here goes ….

Brace yourself as we move into the dark side of football. I am now going to share what probably constitutes the worst aspect of the sport - to be named as the reserve! To be more clear, I'm not talking about the situation where some spoilt brat starts the game, before being replaced by a reserve. Or, as my son's manager calls it, to 'have a rest'. Now, I am sure that being given 'a rest' can be disappointing. However, at least you originally were the first pick and someone else was considered to be worse than yourself i.e. replacing you, whilst you 'rest'. I'm talking about being 'selected' to be reserve. At my school, this meant having your name on the school noticeboard alongside the number 12. For everyone to see. In my case, for a full season! By the end of the season this was tantamount to public humiliation. In front of the public you most valued i.e. your mates and footballing peers.

In my day - did I really say that? - being selected as twelfth man was even less attractive than today. In my school you were not referred to as a 'reserve' but as 'not picked'. Flashback to 'my day' (again!): "Shez have you seen the team sheet for Saturday?" I ask. "Yes, YOU (emphasis heard even if not meant), were 'not picked'" replies Shez (the brother of one of the teachers on the selection committee). To add insult to injury, Shez was increasingly picked instead of me. I'm sure it had nothing to do with his brother being a teacher at the school. Nothing at all. Honest (usually means you're lying).

To be clear, 'not picked', was not the relatively pleasant 'not being picked'. Where your name did not appear on the team sheet and after a short, sharp, shock you could console yourself with thoughts of spending Saturday morning watching Tiswas. This was the full blown 'not-picked-and-you-will-miss-Tiswas' because you are going on the coach to Halifax to watch Sir's brother play instead of you for a full ninety minutes'. Yes, you read it right, ninety.

Nowadays, being one of the many reserves on the bench is de riguer. At local league they have even introduced rolling subs to accommodate this modern approach to not making the first eleven. In my day (again!), you were a lone wolf and you weren't guaranteed a run out. Despite missing Tiswas.

Remember recording something to watch it later was not an option in those days.

Many a time I returned home with a clean strip. Or, to be more accurate, with a strip that was as 'clean' as when I'd set off (my Mum had left home by then). I did however, usually return home, to packet soup that my Dad had 'made'. And if 'we' were playing at home - rather than places I had never been before like Bury, Bolton, Manchester - I sometimes even caught the tail end of Tiswas.

So how did this come to be? At Burnley Grammar School (non fee-paying before you start) we had a good team. I think I'm right in saying that our year won the Lancashire Under 16's. Pupils started at 'the Grammar School' in the third year of their secondary school education. From memory, in the third year, I was the regular centre half. Mainly, because I was then relatively tall. As centre half, my job was to head the ball back towards their goalkeeper, after he had kicked it as far as he could. I saw myself as a Gordon McQueen type, complete with his long hair, which did me no favours with the selection committee. My other 'attribute'[9] was that I gave no quarter. One particular memory being my decision to take out a 'bearded' Blackpool giant, right in front of Sir, after watching him bully most of our team. I remember Sir (Stevie Cool – pictured in the

---

[9] wrong word as I have never been particularly good at heading which I wish they would have spotted earlier

photo gallery) recanting the episode to the town team scout
– the 'nearest' I ever got to playing for the town. I digress
but it is my book after all.

So I had been getting in the team, until one day, something
happened that led to being number 12 for the rest of the
season and I seem to remember the all of the following
season.

From memory, Adrian Hirst joined our school mid-way
through the first year. He came from living 'abroad'. What
I do remember – like it was yesterday – was that we were
playing a game at Barden School and Kevin Singh (think of
a goalie the size and resemblance of the massive native
American from One Flew Over The Cuckoo's Nest)
launched one of his big kicks towards our defence. I was on
the side lines (pertinent) when I saw something that I will
take to my grave.

As the Chief's kick came down from the sky - past some
geese – Adrian Hirst **took the ball on his chest**, before it
had bounced, bringing it down to his feet, before making a
lovely pass. I was gobsmacked, impressed and assured that I
had witnessed a life-changing event from my new home on
the sideline. And I was right.

Nowadays, 'Aidy' is Chairman / Manager / Player of
Waddington FC. Which sounds like a modern version of
Brian Glover in Kes, with Aidy doing the equivalent of

picking himself to be Bobby Charlton, then giving himself a penalty before allowing himself to retake it so that he scores.

So how did this year-long humiliation leave me feeling? Below is the stream of conscience notes I originally made when returning to this chapter of my life. I have left them as they were initially put down (a mixture of lower and upper case) as it captures my current thinking and means that I do not need to delve deeper into how I thought then.

EXPLAIN THE FEELINGS AND THOUGHTS OF GOING AWAY AND HOME WITHOUT EVEN COMING ON MOST GAMES, LONG JOURNEYS TO PLACES LIKE HALIFAX, BURY, MANCHESTER, DRIVEN BY MY DADS ASSURANCE THAT IF I KEPT AT IT MY CHANCE WOULD COME, A BIT EMBARRASSED TO GET ON THE BUS, A BIT WANTING TO PLAY FOR THE SECONDS WHERE I WOULD GET 'GAME TIME' (A PHRASE I HAVE ONLY RECENTLY STARTED USING – EXPLANATION LATER), SLOWLY RECOGNISING THAT MY ROLE SEEMED TO BE TO KEEP PEOPLE ENTERTAINED ON THE BUS

I REMEMBER STEVIE COOL COMING UP AT THE END OF THE SEASON TO THANK ME / EXPLAIN WHY I HAD BEEN A NON PLAYING SUB FOR MOST OF THE SEASON. I WISH I COULD REMEMBER WHAT HE SAID. I ALSO, JUST ABOUT REMEMBER,

DARREN TAYLOR (who I believe went onto to get double blues at either Cambridge or Oxford – the son of a collier worker - OUR CAPTAIN AND ON REFLECTION THE NEAREST THING I HAD TO A PEER HERO) showing some concern. The rest of the team, appeared equally embarrassed about the situation, whilst I stuck at it (probably firm in my Dad's belief that I would get my opportunity).

So how did this all come to pass? For some reason I seem to have buried this footballing story. I need greater information. Time to call my Dad, to talk footy. Unusually started by myself. Hopefully my Dad can remember something useful.

So I ring my Dad on a Sunday afternoon – not the norm – hoping that he can shed some light. He informs me that he only has two memories about my "illustrious playing career". Firstly, he remembers turning up to watch me and the teacher telling him that "I had the turning circle of the Queen Mary"[10]. To make sure I fully understood what the teacher had told my Dad, he puts his own spin on it, "you were a little bit cumbersome." He never gets to his second memory of my illustrious playing career, as he got distracted

---

[10] Queen Mary! Not even something glamorous, like The Titanic. I believe Don Revie referred to one of his centre halves – Paul Madeley – as 'his Rolls Royce'. Maybe the teacher thought the Queen Mary had been fitted with Rolls Royce engines?

by reminding me how good my brother was[11] before moving onto what stopped his playing career (a broken wrist tackling someone who went on to playing for Preston and Liverpool).

As I write, history seems to be repeating itself, in that my son also appears to rarely plays ninety minutes . Unless he makes a change, like I eventually did. For evidence see John Dewhurst's sageful referral to myself as Zico in end of season school report in the photo gallery. .

---

[11] He takes pleasure in informing my friends that one of his sons (Warrick) was a good player, whilst his other son (Blair) could have been a good player. I will leave it with yourself to analyse which of his three sons is missing.

Chapter 4

Kit

My first kit-related memory involves someone who at the time played for the opposition but later became a good friend of mine: Ian Sheridan (Shez).

It was my first game for Coal Clough Juniors at the famously muddy Cherry Fold. We were playing our local rivals Hargher Clough who played in a kit that was bright orange from top to toe. It was Saturday morning in winter and as we approached the pitch I saw a member of the opposition take a running front-facing dive straight through a big puddle of mud. He then did a 'present' - with arms above head (Casper style) – of his now black down the front kit. On reflection, this is the only graceful thing I can remember seeing Shez do. In gymnastics, he would have scored a perfect ten. I later learned that his Dad – who had played to a reasonable standard – had told him to do it. Advising him that once he was dirty he wouldn't be worried about getting his strip dirty and could concentrate on the game. Good thinking. Especially as Shez took all of their free kicks, corner kicks and goal kicks. I seem to remember that this was because he could kick the ball the furthest. Or, maybe his older brother was also on the selection committee at the Hargher Clough!

I have never been 'Kevin Kit.' The majority of my 'kit' is second hand (see end notes), or more accurately, has been rejected by others. For instance, I currently play in pair of LGBT rainbow coloured socks that my son 'donated' after a year's wear. Despite me not being gay, they are my best pair, in that they match and don't have holes. They are also very easy to identify in a drawer full of formerly white socks and therefore easy to pick out at 8.55 (KO 9pm). They also – and here's a confession – kind of match my turquoise bri-nylon shorts. I secured the shorts from the hospice jumble sale at the end of my street. From memory they cost fifty pence. The shorts are indestructible, although a bit roomy. The latter is quite an achievement given the size of my saddle. The other common denominator amongst my sporting attire, is that once it makes into my kit bag, it ain't going anywhere fast[12]. In fact, the only way out is if I lose it.

The background to my embracement of new-to-me attire is, quelle surprise, my childhood. More specifically my Dad

---

[12] I have a red jumper that a mate (Dickie Davies – not the one with the Mallen streak who read out the results) threw in a bin in Spain in 2000. After recovering the jumper from the bin I regularly wore the jumper for footy, walking, working round the house and lounging, for at least the next six years. This despite the fact that I really don't suit red.

drilling it into me that good kit did not make you a good player. Although, I can confirm that the converse is also true i.e. that having shit kit does not make you a good player either.

Fortunately, my Dad was right and kit doesn't maketh the man. Or to paraphrase the Dalai Lama, 'kit is just possessions'. On reflection, it would appear that I have evolved into an uber non–consumerist. Or, as some of my friends and family mistakenly convey, 'a tight bastard'.

Chapter 5

Players

Players have a range of responsibilities and these change over time. As a child, my favourite player was Tony Currie; a difficult thing to share as a Claret living in Leeds. His job was to be the player that I most wanted to be. To be more specific, the player I most wanted to play like. And, once I was freed from the role of heading the goalkeepers long punt back towards the keeper, Tony Currie[13] was the player I tried to emulate i.e. a slow, creative, midfielder that could bend the ball. My teacher and Dad can confirm that I at least achieved one aspect of Currie's game. Nowadays, the role of my favourite player is to form the spine of my security password. Although in the last few years, I have changed it to Glenn Little, in case any of my Leeds mates found out.

Another role of professional players is to be the 'best player you've ever played against'. In my case this was Billy Ingham aka the Ginger Pele. It was when I was about 16, playing for

---

[13] My Dad and brother however continued to liken me to the then cumbersome Emlyn Hughes

a men's pub team, after I had played for school in the morning. At the time, Billy probably was not at his best, having retired from playing professionally to become one of Burnley's bus drivers. However, I can still remember - on probably the one occasion that he actually tried - him hitting the hyper-space button (remember that?) and dribbling the ball at pace through our midfield and defence. The dribbling, although impressive, was not the surprise. After all, they didn't call him Ginger Pele just because he had heavy hair. What absolutely sticks with me is the raw pace, from someone who was by then an old man. He appeared to be able to dribble considerably faster than he could run. If that makes sense.

The only other person who I have known have this capability (a 5th gear), is my old mate Jeff Brown, who over 10 yards could hit the front of the dinner queue with a speed that defied his physique at the time.

As the number of professional British players declines, so does the likelihood of playing against the Billy Inghams of this world. For instance, in the year that Huddersfield were promoted to the Premiership, their chief executive called in the parents of 100 members of the academy (8 – 16 year olds) to tell them that their association with the club was to end in a month. The club's academy (ranked 12th most 'productive' of the EFL's 72 clubs in 2016) had not brought through one Premiership player since John Stead. He graduated in 1999. You cannot argue with the logic. At the same time, you cannot help but to feel sorry for those juniors that are recruited with less than a 1% chance of ever making it professionally.

Chapter 6

Graft versus craft

The Premiership Player of the Year 2016/17 awards was further proof that the game is losing beauty and has become more about money. How else can you explain the campaign for the hard-working N'Golo Kante to be placed in front of the exciting Dele Alli and the goal-scoring revelation Harry Kane? We are told that the diminutive Frenchman is the equivalent of two players (he works that hard). We are correctly told that his hard work frees up the more creative players - like the beautiful Hazard – to be attack-minded.

So why might the hard-working Kante be valued higher than Hazard who is reputed to be the next Messi? It only makes sense in a footballing world where money is more important than entertainment.

I don't dispute that there is a subliminal logic to Kante winning the Player of the Year award i.e. his hard work decreases the risk of not making the Champions League and therefore decreases the risk of not being able to pay the wages of your Champions League players. However, why should this logic trump the logic of electing the most exciting and beautiful player within the Premier League the winner? Of which there are still a few candidates, despite managers increasingly micro-managing expression out of our game.

As I say to my footballing friends, no-one comes to watch me work, and I don't want to go and watch someone else work. Now I am not saying that I do not value hard graft. For instance, it has been a big part of my own game. However, it is daft to put graft above the craft of the beautiful game. The 'fans' that collude with this hard work approach are the same ones that say that they'd prefer to see their team win 'ugly' than lose gracefully. Work over craft. Win at all cost. To these fans – one of whom has stood or sat in front of me for at least thirty years – I politely suggest that you go away with an F.

SECTION 2

WATCHING OUR GAME

Me watching Burnley –everyone's favourite second team –
beat Barcelona on the TV

Although I have done more than my fair share of watching football, if I am being honest, it is my least favourable aspect of the game. On reflection, it is probably because unlike playing, talking or singing about football, you cannot usually influence the game you are watching. Unless you stopping watching it. Consequently, with watching there comes a risk that it will be boring. Or in other words – using an old fashioned footballing concept – it may not be entertaining.

That said, in the last forty years I have seen 'some' entertaining football. Although, I sense that I would have witnessed far more entertainment had I watched the game and Burnley in the forty-year period before I started. However, we are where we are and I am not going to give up watching the game. Especially as I have spent over £100 on a pair of glasses so that I can see who scores.

Chapter 7

Watching your first ever live game

We can all remember our first game. Mine was a full house at Turf Moor for Burnley against Liverpool. Like you I can remember the noise, the excitement, the being with your Dad and the most people you have ever seen. We sat in the newly opened Bob Lord Stand and I remember the claret and blue Burnley flag flying from the top of it. I remember looking across at the ram-jam-packed Longside - half full of Burnley fans and half full of Scousers - and being scared. We had Leighton James (before Derby bought him for the record British transfer fee) and they had Kevin Keegan (one of two English players to win the Ballon D'Or in my time of watching football, name the other[14]).

One of my abiding memories – and I have never experienced it since – was the crowd excitement lifting every time that James got the ball on the wing. And he played in front of us in the first half. However, the thing I remember the most, was Tommy Smith (who must have been 'marking' James)

---

[14] Michael Owen in 2001. Keegan won it twice – 1978 and 1979

picking the ball up to take a throw in directly in front of me and my Dad. At which stage my Dad shouted out to the hard man of football: "Smith, you big pudding." To which, Smith (ball in one hand) turned round and out of the back of his hand told my Dad to "fuck off!" Tommy Smith, swore, at my Dad! I remember walking back up Centenary Way after the game and thinking, the Inghams have arrived on the world stage of football.

Chapter 8

Watching with a mate who supports the opposition

It's Burnley v Everton, 12.30 kick off on Saturday. Bobby is not going, so I ask along a friend who is a lifelong Everton supporter – having checked with the lads I sit with first. This is a first for me and them. A guest away supporter in the Longside!

I inform John that I can offer him safe passage. John is one of a family of Evertonians. His Dad and his four brothers, all follow Everton. He has no sisters and his surname is accurate - Male.

We meet in the Cricket Club beforehand. As per, it is full of away supporters. John is loving it. Neither team has been doing well. Burnley have not won in the last twelve games and Everton are doing equally as poorly. However, we are still 7th and if Everton win today they go equal with us on points and they restart their efforts to claim a position in Europe. Everton supporters are predicting a draw. As per, I predict a one-nil Burnley win. On reflection, neither I,

Doey, Pete and more recently Adrian, have ever predicted anything other than a Burnley win. And I mean ever. Although I seem to remember Pete once predicted a draw. He of little faith.

We take 'our' seats in the Longside. For the first time ever, an away supporter sat next to me in my son's seat. Interest is added by Michael Keane (an acquaintance of my friend's daughter) making his first return to Turf Moor. Plus Aaron Lennon (who another acquaintance had taught) playing against the team we recently bought him from. Quite soon Everton go ahead. John manages to limit his celebration to a smile. My feelings are less restrained - the usual coating of expletives - underwritten by the knowledge that we never win when we go behind. Also, it had not escaped my attention that I would be sitting next to an away supporter, for the rest of the game!

I then have a Damascene moment and I confidently informed everyone around us that we will win 2 v 1. Further, that for every goal we score, I will be providing my Everton colleague with a hug: "So he doesn't feel left out." Well to cut a lovely game short, Burnley score the next two goals. John gets two lovely big hugs and this is the first time under Dyche that Burnley have gone onto to win a Premiership game after conceding the first goal. First time in 52 games! However, it is not the first time that Victor The Predictor (one of my self-appointed none de plumes) has got it right. I say it again, Burnley 2 v Everton 1.

As we leave the Longside I inform my fellow Longsiders that I have watched the game with an Everton (pointing John out) and that I would try and bring a Chelsea to the next home game. For good luck. I quickly think to myself that I may have hit onto something and that it is will be worth renewing Bobby's concessionary season ticket.

As per, we retire to the Cricket Club, for post-match refreshments and to watch on the TV where we are in the league. This, in my book (literally), is one of the few appropriate uses of the TV for football. The TV shows that we are still 7th and we are closing on Arsenal for 6th. At the bar an Everton supporter informs us that we should be aiming for Europe. He also shares stories of the good times he and his mates have had this season following his team in Europe. Unfortunately, today's result means that he would unlikely be watching Everton abroad next season. Generously, he wishes us all the best on our travels. For the first time ever I imagine us playing abroad! I then commit myself to going wherever and whenever it is. To my knowledge, this would make me the first Ingham to watch the Clarets abroad. A small step for man but a big step for Claretkind.

On the way home, in a phone call with a fellow Burnley supporter, I share the excitement of possibly watching Burnley abroad. He brings me up to speed by saying 'don't worry, we're buying a bus'.

Chapter 9

Watching the best player you have ever seen with your own eyes

To be clear - this is not something I should have to explain - this means live and not on the TV!

Obviously this section can be broken down into sub-genres. So here goes: *Best performing seal* - Beckham dropping it on a sixpence from over half the length of the pitch to opposing wings; *consistently a better player than anyone else on the pitch* – trendy Trevor Stevens before he moved to Everton; *best runner with the ball* – either Stevie 'Skippy' Kindon or Cristiano Ronaldo at Man Utd (who ran faster with the ball than anyone I have ever seen run without the ball - despite adding in stepovers); *best single handed match winning performance* – Beckham for England v Greece at Old Trafford; *best tackler* – Steve Brown Wednesday night 5 –a-side regular and his flying indoor slide tackles; *heaviest tackler* – Mr Emott (your family felt it) teacher at Burnley Grammar; *hardest shot* – Mr Smith at Coal Clough juniors; *best Cruyff back pass to a goalie* – yours truly; *best player* – Stoichkov; *favourite player* when a kid - Tony Currie; favourite player when a young man

– Aidy Randall and Glenn Little; *favourite player when an adult* – George Boyd.

BTW, it may not have escaped your notice that that all of my favourite players lacked pace but had finesse. Choosing your favourite player appears to be like choosing a dog i.e. you select one that looks like you.

Chapter 10

Watching Burnley 1 v Watford 0

A pretty nondescript game to an almost full house. We go joint 5th and I am one of the few Burnley followers that applauds Andre Gray's return (whilst welcoming everyone else's rendition of 'there's only one greedy bastard, there's only one greedy bastard, one greedy bastard, there's only one greedy bastard').

However, it is a game that I will always remember, for the view i.e. a three-person gap in the seats directly in front of me. For the last 10 years or so this gap – in the upper tier of the Longside - has been filled by Doey (school friend), Pete (Doey's brother in law) and Malcolm (Doey's father in law).

For the record, Doey is the person that I have watched Burnley Football Club with the most in my life. Pete will not be far behind, as the Last Day of the Longside cover picture confirms. The picture shows us on the Longside, twenty-two years ago, Burnley v Hull City in the second division. The picture shows Doey and Pete stood in front of me. Exactly the same arrangements as our current one, with

Doey directly in front of me and Pete to his immediate right. In terms of watching Burnley with Doey, you can go back at least another 15 years before 1996. Malcolm, who is in his 70s, is a lovely bloke who provides us with boiled sweets each game.

As Adrian and myself got settled down for the start of the Watford game, I looked at the three empty seats in front of us and informed Adrian that something was not right. I explained how Malcolm had said at the previous game that he was going in for a bit of chemotherapy but that did not explain why Doey and Pete were not here.

After a while, I said what I was thinking. "I bet Malcolm has died today." This was the only reason that I could imagine all three of them not being here. At half time, I asked some of the lads if they knew anything. One of them let me call Doey as I'd left my phone at home. No answer! Something's wrong.

When I got back to our seats, the woman who sits next to Pete informed me that she had seen Pete in town during the week, and he had mentioned Malcolm's chemo. "Something wrong" I could not stop saying it. "I don't know why all three of them are not here" I reiterated. I wondered about sitting in their seats, for the second half, in solidarity. I will always remember watching the game through the gap of those three empty seats; thinking: 'there's something wrong! Where's Doey and Pete?'

When I got home and to my phone, I called Doey and he told me that Malcolm had a heart attack that lunch-time and had died. Bobby heard me speaking with Doey. 'Has someone died Dad?', 'Yes, Bobby'. We revisited my observation that something had to be wrong as Pete and Doey never miss a game. Bobby looked shocked 'That's sad Dad.' 'I know it is Bobby'. I texted Doey and then his wife. I let Adrian know what happened. I decided that from now on, I will always take boiled sweets to the game, in memory of Malcolm. Regrettably I have not always done so.

Chapter 11

Watching on the television

As I write, I am cogitating whether to watch today's Burnley v Liverpool on the TV, in my local pub. Or whether to watch it at the home of the fella I sit next to at the Turf (he has Sky). The background to the deliberation is that I am expecting us to get a good tubbing and watching it in public comes with an element of risk. Especially as the landlord of my local is a Liverpool fan and somehow (now this 'is' completely wrong) my local in Leeds has become known as a Liverpool pub. However, the alternative – watching it in a safe environment – feels a bit of a cop out.

My thinking includes a view that a proper Burnley lad should man-up to a potential public humiliation. A lesser consideration is that, at the risk of sounding egotistical, it will make the game more enjoyable for the Liverpool fans present to have Burnley Lee to laugh at. And finally, but probably the most important / unlikely. Should little Burnley beat the mighty Liverpool .... just imagine the amount of solid piss that I could extract in this Liverpool pub.

Another option is to watch the first half at my mate's house (which is not far from my local) and then assess the lie of the land, before making a decision about where to watch the second half.

I share this though- process because it is an example of how football is a central part of 'our' lives and this is just deciding where to watch the game on the telly! I say 'our' lives, safe in the knowledge that there will be Liverpool supporters (including the pub landlord) thinking, I hope that Burnley Lee does, or does not, come in to watch the game.

So, the pub it is then!

My favourite memory from watching football on television is when Stan Bowles has the ball at his feet somehow way ahead of the rest of his team, isolated like a lone trumpeter playing reveille. He was just inside the sideline at Loftus Park. Alongside him is a big burley defender squat down, side-ways, showing him the touchline, fearful that he was about to be skinned. As Stan waited for the rest of his team to join him, almost stationary, he threw the defender a couple of casual dummies. Dropping his shoulder, ever so slightly moving his hips and feigning that he may take the defender on. The timing is wonderful in that the game has almost come to a stand-still, except for the brain of the defender who is concentrating on the feet of Bowles. The filming is perfect in that it focusses on just the two players and the desolate space around them. Bowles, matador like, throws the defender a third fake dummy and the bull pounces, scything Bowles to the ground. Stan gets up and laughs. His work was done. Now I am regaling this from distant memory. I have tried locating the clip on you tube but to no avail. If you find it then please let me know. There's a pint in it.

Chapter 12

Watching on the wireless whilst ironing

Yes, you read it right.

Tuesday night, Burnley v Leeds in the Carabao Cup. Should I or shouldn't I go over to Burnley for the game? A big decision because I'd like to watch the recently recruited Leeds signings - Chris Wood and Charlie Taylor - play for Burnley. Plus, it would strengthen my hand in post-match assessment, if I can say that I'd been there. Plus (again) if I do not go, a friend that is a Leeds supporter will not be able to go as he needs me to buy him a ticket in the Burney end. After much deliberation I surprise myself and decide not to go.

Eventually I find the 'correct' radio station (Radio Lancashire not available) and I start to listen. Burnley are in the ascendancy, even ex-Leeds United playing Noel Whelan (my son goes to the same school as he did) recognises this. However, with eight minutes to go - half through ironing one of my work shirts - Sako scores a 'great' (Whelan's word) goal. Although the other commentator ('Popey') is off message and says that "it luckily went through the Burnley keeper's legs."

Burnley go back on attack and, penalty! Burnley elect the £15 million Wood to take the penalty. In front of the Leeds travelling, he scores in the 89th minute. Boom! Then, 3 minutes into extra time, Leeds are awarded a penalty. 1 v 2! 6th minute of extra time, Robbie Brady curls one in from a free kick. 2 v 2. Extra time and I now move onto ironing my work trousers. There are no additional goals in extra time and I jettison the ironing to move onto the laptop to start writing it up. Yes. How modern can you get? Listening to the footie on the radio whilst writing. Penalties. WhatsApp, Facebook and text messages from my Leeds friends have gone quiet. My phone has stopped pinging.

First penalty, both teams score. Second penalty, both teams score. Third penalty both team score. After each Leeds goal Whelan shouts "get in!" Fourth penalty we (a centre half) miss! They score the next 2. Jammie Bastards! Glad I didn't go!

The phone starts pinging. There's a battle between text messages and Facebook postings to see which can get to me the most. This is the first time I can remember 'watching' my team on the opposition's radio station. You probably don't realise it but national radio is relatively neutral – unless self-appointed hardman Alan Green is commentating at a Liverpool game. Listening to Noel Whelan comment on Radio Leeds makes me realise how parochial commentators can be. If you don't believe me, let me share Noel's observation that "the Burnley fans are no longer clapping with all three of their hands."

In the badinage that followed the Burnley v Leeds cup game – and there was plenty – I adopt a clever response. I try to throw them off the scent by saying that I, also had been part rooting for Leeds (their ears pricked up), as everyone loves a giant killer! I then went on the customary offensive by reminding them of a few stats i.e. they had 7 shots on goal and 6 of them had been from penalties. I also reminded them that the remaining 'shot on goal' had come from outside the box and had gone through our deputising goalie's legs. I was not sure whether the stats were true but people seemed to buy it.

After the game, I read an interview with Leeds centre half Pontus Jansson; whom I rate. He stated that he had taken it upon himself to explain to new arrivals at the club, that "Leeds is a team that a lot of people hate in this country. I've seen that. People hate Leeds for a reason. Because Leeds were a fantastic club in the past." He went on to say that he'd played for Malmo who were also hated in Sweden "because Malmo are too good for the others and that can be the reason for Leeds also." Pontus, in the unlikely event that you read this book, it may be true for Malmo but – at the risk of stating the very obvious – it isn't the reason why some people 'hate' Leeds.

If Pontus wants to do his job properly, he may want to talk to opposition supporters about Leeds. For instance, he may want to talk to older football supporters (pre me). They will explain how the club became 'dirty Leeds' because of the way that they earned their initial success under Revie i.e. boring and aggressive football. Or he may want to speak about younger supporters who will inform you about the aggression of their supporters. For instance, I attended the Bradford game where they had lifted the ban on Leeds away support. At the game, Leeds fans injured one another and put through the windows of their own buses. On the windy journey back to the train station, I heard hardened Leeds supporters say that they would never follow their team again. Maybe Pontus should speak with them.

I take no pleasure in writing this. As far as I am concerned, Leeds supporters are part of the footballing brotherhood. I do not hate Leeds. I no longer even hate Blackburn Rovers aka Bastard Rovers. So why would I hate Leeds? In fact, at the risk of sounding patronising, I feel sorry for them because I have watched how they have been mistreated by their so-called owners. For instance, Bates taking the commentary of Leeds games off the local BBC radio station. Or Cellino threatening to stop Leeds supporters watching their club at away games. Or the constant changing of their fixtures to accommodate armchair customers. In my opinion, football still belongs to us and that includes Leeds United supporters.

Chapter 13

Watching as a customer, fan or supporter?

Customer

Oxford Dictionary definition *of* **customer** - *a person who buys goods or services from a shop or business.*

I am sat in the East End of London, having a few beers the night before the London Marathon. I watch as the TV cameras show Spurs fans/customers flocking down Wembley Way in droves, leaving a good ten minutes before the end of the game. My initial thought is that people are off to an organised fight between fans. But oh no, not something working class like football violence. The following week I read that the early exit was evidence of 'embourgeoisification' - a worldy in Scrabble. The very word itself is a signal of how football has changed.

Further evidence can be found in the increasing trend for people to act as customers and leave the game early. These early-exiting people seem to be treating the game as a good or service that they can be dropped if it does not meet their customer expectations. In one way, I suppose it is the logical progression of football increasingly treating itself as a business.

The Champions League and the format it is played in is a good example of the consumerisation of the midweek game. I refuse to be a customer of this shite good / service. Furthermore, I do not want the Champions League to be sullying this book.

Since at least 2014, I have hoped that the Champions League will become a league of McDonald-type-brands, that field Harlem Globetrotter-type teams, who shuffle off and let us have our game back. I also hope that the Champions League will move to China, along with all the fancy dan owners, players and 'customers'. Obviously, the Europa League is a different proposition – now that Burnley have qualified[15].

Fan

Oxford Dictionary definition of **fan** - a person who has a strong interest in or admiration for a particular person or thing. Its origin is late 19th century (originally US): abbreviation of fanatic.

In my opinion, the term 'fan' is often misused. Often by foreign managers who misinterpret 'fans' as being the top of the family tree because of their enthusiasm. In my world, to re-use Dyche's phrase, '100% effort is the absolute minimum'. The difference between 'fans' and 'supporters' is that the latter not only have

---

[15] Written before we nobly decided – in the words of Bullseye – 'to let someone else have a go at winning Bully's main prize'.

the effort levels of 'fans' but they also have the nous to go the extra yard and think about the bigger picture. It is not what their club can do for them but also what they can do for their club.

Despite my ongoing commitment and passion for Burnley Football Club I don't think I have ever been a 'fan'. If I ever was, I plan to ensure that I am no longer. Especially now that I have learned that 'fan' is a word that comes from America.

Fans are like enthusiastic teenagers; everything is a drama and it all about them. They ring into football phone-ins crying about how horrible it is that 'their' (sic) team have not won silverware this week. The manager must go and more money must be spent.

Fans are also haters. They hate opposing fans, players, managers, owners and referees. Fans' hatred of others often seems greater than their love of their own club. A while ago I came to the conclusion that I do not need to hate Blackburn Rovers in order to love my club. In fact, I sometimes even call them 'Rovers', instead of 'Bastards'. I say this as someone who recognises that Burnley's hatred of Blackburn Rovers was probably the one thing that helped keep our support together throughout the 80's and 90's. In this fallow period, where our lower league status meant that we did not play them for 18 seasons, we sang as many songs about how much we hated 'Bastards', as we sang about our support for our own club. In the 80's and 90's our raison d'etre was to one day play Blackburn and beat them (on and off the field[16]).

Nowadays, my love for my club and our game, is greater than hate or wanting to appear fanatical. It is more important. It is support for my club and our game.

Supporter

Oxford Dictionary definition of *supporter* - a person who is actively interested in and wishes success for a particular sports team. The dictionary provides an illustration i.e. "an Oxford United supporter." I am glad to hear that the Oxford dictionary is written by a local.

As mentioned, I consider myself to be a supporter. For instance, I have never left a Burnley game early. I will never walk out on my team. Although my support was tested to the max in the nineties when a 0 v 5 home defeat on the Saturday was followed by a mid-week tonking by Manchester City 0 v 6[17]. As the

---

[16] I will never forget the incredible pre-match atmosphere at Turf Moor when we eventually played them. Yet be careful what you wish for. We were defeated 0 v 2 then 5 v 0 and the second humbling was on April Fool's Day!

[17] In verifying my recollection I discovered that I had forgotten something that made it even worse. Five days after the 0v6 we hosted our local rivals Preston in our third consecutive home league game and were defeated 0v1. Even worser (the right word

Longside emptied to the sound of 'Blue Moon', from an army of City supporters, I had to grip hold of my seat to stop myself going. I clearly remember turning to Jeff Brown and saying 'stay and we will remember this day forever'. This is the behaviour of supporters.

Supporters are reliable, long-standing volunteers. We literally 'support' our team. For instance, when both Burnley and myself were in a less favourable financial position, I remember paying for season tickets, pies, drinks etc and saying to other supporters: "it's ok, it all goes to a good cause, it all goes to the club." And I meant it.

We must be the only volunteers that pay to volunteer. And what is even madder is that we even volunteer to support other 'sports teams'; such as the lower league clubs that we go and watch when our teams are not playing. For instance, I sometimes go and watch Guiseley FC and I once even supported our pub team, who were possibly worse than our pub cricket team (who I play for).

'Supporters' also do not want to see their team win at all costs. Well this one doesn't. Believe it or not I love football and I like to see it played well. Whilst I recognise the need

---

in the instance) Kurt Nogan (ex-claret) scored the only goal. I defy anyone to have watched a worse run of home defeats in 2 weeks. 0 v 12! What I am struggling to remember is how I attended all three games, whilst living away and having very little money .

for teams to work hard (especially the current Burnley team) I want to be entertained. I would rather see a good and entertaining game than see my team winning a boring one. Contrary to football opinion this does not make me less of a supporter but it probably makes me less of a fan. Which – as already discussed – is just fine by me.

No one like to see a man lose his job but as a football supporter it was refreshing to see WBA get rid of Pulis. Not because they were at risk of relegation, but because supporters were sick of watching boring football. I heard one Baggies supporter say that he'd rather see them get relegated playing good football then stay up at all costs. In the Guardian, Paul Doyle captured Pulis's no-frills efforts to keep the club in the Premier League: 'No one goes to the cinema to watch the news'. Or, in my own words, a comment I have shared with fellow supporters: 'No one pays to watch me work, why should I pay to watch someone else work?' Compare Pulis's football with Guardiola's 'freedom with responsibility' approach. I was looking forward to Man City coming to Turf Moor. I did not enjoy WBA's visit under Pulis.

I will finish this chapter by sharing a story about football supporters (again regaled in the preferred footballing first person). It's Burnley's last away game of the 2017/18 season and Wenger's last game at the Emirates, Burnley are getting beat 5 v 0, and they join the Arsenal supporters in singing: "One Arsene Wenger, there's only one Arsene Wenger ….." Now that's what I call 'supporters' rather than 'fans' or 'customers'.

SECTION THREE

TALKING ABOUT OUR GAME

Me, multi-tasking i.e. talking footy and drinking beer

I remember an old fella telling me that "you're never lost as long as you've got a tongue in your head." I have discovered that this is especially true if the head also has football in it. In my experience, you can meet people (okay men), in most places in the world and within the response to one question (who's your team?) the ice is well and truly broken. A second rhetorical question (e.g. you won't like Blackburn then will you?) can result in you making a new BFE. A third question (do you go and watch them?) and you know whether the bloke has integrity. Even the men that do not like football usually have a football story. And I can imagine no bigger an accolade than sharing my observation that talking about football can even make some men listen! A rare thing indeed. However, an understandable rarity, as by comparison with taking about football, listening is equivalent to having to take your turn to be goalkeeper.

Chapter 14

Talking with your Dad

The longest and most challenging football conversations I have ever had are with my Dad. Maybe not surprising given his passion for, and my interest, in the game. I conservatively estimate that we have spent at least 1000 waking hours 'discussing' football; over the phone alone! To put that in context, if you allow seven hours for sleeping and ablutions, that means 59 full days 'talking' about football. Or, the duration of 571 ninety minute games; including talking right through your pint, pie and a pee break at half time. This is the longest chapter in the book for reasons that will become self-evident.

Now to be more accurate, when I say 'discussing' football or 'talking' about football, I really mean 'listening'[18] to my Dad share his footballing-world-view. Since I left Burnley – more than thirty years ago – I have spoken with my Dad most weeks on the phone. The average phone call has usually been

---

[18] On reflection, maybe this chapter should be in another section called 'listening'.

around the length of a standard game of 5–a-side and the thing we have 'talked' about most has been football. He tells me this is because he is passionate about our game. This is something I can confirm. Although, to be honest, his passion is something that had escaped my attention – probably because I have never known any different.

Within the broad subject that is football, the dominant theme has been how rubbish my Dad considers football to be nowadays. Within this genre, his focus has mainly been on a sub-genre of how Burnley are particularly rubbish. Including their manager, players and supporters. Throughout these conversations it would appear to have escaped my Dad's notice that he is speaking to a season ticket holder at Burnley Football Club.

Particularly frustrating is that my Dad watched Burnley when they were the best club in the land and when the team was graced by the best player Burnley has probably ever had in Jimmy McIlroy. Whilst for the last forty years I have mainly watched Burnley in the lower leagues with no misconceptions about how rubbish Burnley have been to watch e.g. we went 23 Championship games undefeated in the 2015 / 16 season but I did not see one entertaining performance throughout the season. The irony is, that I agree with my Dad that football is by comparison less entertaining and I have thought that for over forty years; as evidenced by my favourite players still being the likes of Tony Currie, Frank Worthington, Duncan McKenzie, Peter Barnes, Stan Bowles….. Some of my Dad's favourites

To those not in the know, you may have thought that watching Burnley for the last forty years, would have provided me with competitive advantage over my Dad, who has watched them a handful of times over the same period. Especially, as I have been sitting next to my Dad at each of the handful of games that he has attended. However, you'd be wrong. For, as my Dad explains, he has not been brainwashed like those people that watch Burnley every week and he can see what is really happening. Credit to my Dad, given the circumstances, he has developed a good debating approach i.e. less is more.

On reflection, my Dad's assessment of Burnley's rubbishness seems to coincide with my Dad stopping watching Burnley in the 70's[19]. 'Coincidentally' their rubbishness seems to coincide with me starting to watch them. I'm no Sigmund Freud, but what's that about?

Obviously, despite football being rubbish, my Dad still watches about three games a week on the TV (he's got Sky and BT Sport). Plus, he never misses Match Of The Day (ideally without knowing the scores). Obviously, despite Burnley being rubbish, he has continued following Burnley through the newspaper, radio, TV and most recently live through a written commentary, on a website, on his girlfriend's iPad! I'd love to see him do this as he hates computers and all that they stand for.

---

[19] Strangely we have never discussed why he stopped going to watch Burnley

The general format for our hour-long phone conversations is an opening five minutes of family chit chat. A gentle warm-up. Then the kick-off is normally started by my Dad blowing the whistle. 'Did you by any chance see that game the other night?' 'No Dad' a quickly snubbed attempt to get the game called off. Bye the way, it took me at least 20 years to adopt this stance and it took my Dad a mere 20 seconds to brush it off. My Dad then spends 20 minutes (if I keep quiet, 30 minutes if I talk) explaining how a game you did not see illustrates one of his pet subjects: big teams are shite, managers are a joke, professional footballers can no longer tackle / use their left foot / head the ball. Strangely enough he makes very few references to referees (he'd be lost in Rugby League). And then, if you have the audacity to offer counter argument. "Lee I 'watch' the game, every minute, every kick." Ergo, I know what I am talking about, meanwhile could you please get on with your job of listening and quietly agreeing in the few moments that I stop for breath. Or if he thinks you are not listening properly, can I do the right thing and accept his incitement to a verbal joust.

Themes that we have spent hours on include: his undying support for the underdog; the poorness of our national team; over-coaching preventing players expressing themselves; conspiracy theories (less frequent in the last ten years) such as Burnley FC purposefully seeking draws in cup games in order to secure the gate receipts from a return fixture. More recently, he has been asking me if I have seen some brilliant lower league game or underdog versus goliath cup game?

Whether I have or not, he then follows up this faux question, with an explanation of how good or unlucky the underdog was. The subtext being – I think - that the game could still be good, if it wasn't rubbish!

If my Dad is struggling to get through my park-the-bus approach to preventing him from talking football, his last resort is to ask himself a hypothetical question. A favourite being "do you know what I would do if I was Burnley Manager?" The answer is always how he would motivate them for a specific game, despite him starting the discussion with the observation that they should not need any motivation for that game.

I regret to say that for the last few years my response has been both passive- aggressive and disingenuous. I now quickly remind him that football is rubbish and consequently I do not want to talk about it. Foolishly hoping this would inspire a change of subject. However, this does not work, for two significant reasons. Firstly, the next-to-last thing that he wants is for someone to agree with him. Secondly, the last thing that he wants is not to talk about football. Apologies Dad if I have placed these in the wrong order. As frustrating as these 'conversations' can be, I am increasingly aware that I will miss his monologues once they have stopped.

Chapter 15

Talking with your Son:

The one person I'd like to talk to more about football seems uninterested, which does not bode well in regard to football continuing to be 'ours' i.e. the Inghams. Bobby's lack of interest in football - other than playing it – is monumental. For instance, I am not sure he has a favourite footballer and if he did I could not tell you who he was. Similarly, he would not be able to tell you mine. Maybe this is a consequence of him being a strong adherent to the 'play not watch' approach to football. Maybe I just don't give him enough space to talk about football. Or maybe, he has not got much to say. Whatever the reasons there can be no larger contrast than comparison between the two Dad and Son football conversations. As evidenced by the respective lengths of each chapter.

As the football chant goes Bobby: "Is this a library? Is this a library?"

Chapter 16

Talking in the pub

Since starting to write this book, I have begun to write down other people's thoughts about football. More specifically I have asked the lads (how much longer can we get away with that?) in the pub who is the best player that they have seen with their own eyes and who is their footballing hero. Below is a selection, in no particular order:

Nev (older fella that I used to drink with on Sunday afternoon before he was run over, his wife died and he ended up in a nursing home): Best player - Tom Finney. Apparently he signed for Preston North End for the price of an old white five-pound note. When Finney took it home his Dad asked: 'where did you steal that from?' Nev informed me that you had to fold up a white fiver to get it in your wallet. Being curious, I asked him how large a white fiver was? To which Nev replied that he was not sure, as at the time he could not have afforded the wallet to put it in, never mind the white fiver. I digress. But that's allowed when talking in the pub (which I will be covering in my next book: 'Ours: The Pub').

Al the Landlord: probably the most surprising answer that I can remember. He is player- manager of a football team and quite knowledgeable. His response, after some deliberation (I imagined he was mulling over whether to choose King Kenny or a more recent candidate like Suarez) was Aldridge. I thought he must have answered the wrong question. He must have thought I asked best player you have played against. However, he went onto explain that it was watching a veterans 5-a-side tournament.

Brett who is a rare animal in that he has never played football and plans – despite my best efforts[20] - to leave it that way. He looks like Jurgen Klopp and has Klopp's enthusiasm for the game despite his lack of knowledge of it. It was with this enthusiasm that he returned from the toilets excited to share a story with the final score crowd i.e. a group of us who sometimes meet on Saturday to listen to the final results and talk football with the 5.30 kick off in the background. Brett explained how on the way back from the toilet he had got talking with a mutual mate and had shared my excitement about Burnley's increased possibility of going to Europe, to which the mutual mate replied, "Why, have they written a song?" We love football but it is even better when combined with two of the other great loves of our life, 'taking the piss'

---

[20] Wanted to make him the Captain of the Lancashire v Yorkshire 11 a side I organised for my 50th. The score was Lancashire 10 v Yorkshire 1 - seeing as you asked. BTW – Yorkshire's goal was offside but the Yorkshire referee gave it!

and 'the pub'. It is for this reason that we gather in Woodies at Saturday tea-time. In the hope that the team of one of our mates gets absolutely tubbed, thus opening the door for faux concern, before opening an even bigger door for laughing-towards-you piss-taking.

In regard to footballing heroes, the responses reflect that I now live and drink in Leeds.

Hobbo, fresh from watching Leeds sneak a five-nil win against Burton Albion, informed me that his hero was John Sheridan. Simply stating that Sheridan was the player that he most wanted to be as he grew up. Standard fayre.

Jim adopted the same logic but as I pointed out - when I'd stopped laughing - 'Terry Cooper' had been a left back. Jim, I salute you for sharing and thinking outside the attackers box.

Mick – who has watched every Leeds United game since 1981, "worldwide" (see end notes) – obtusely chose John Pearson, explaining that he was little known and this was because he had only scored "2 goals in about 80 appearances" for Leeds United. I support the use of the word 'obtuse' by adding that 'JP' was at the time the centre-forward for Leeds Untied. He actually found the net 12 times in 99 appearances but when you deduct the hat-trick against Sheffield United, that leaves 9 in 98. According to Wikipidea, he helped Leeds become second division champions in 1990. I am guessing someone else did the 'heavy lifting'.

Martin adopted a more philosophical approach, he named Jackie Charlton as his footballing hero, elaborating on Jack's off field triumphs. Martin was particularly struck by Jack's response to a question on an Irish chat show. Jack was asked what was his favourite footballing moment? Martin thought he would refer to his involvement in England's 1966 triumph, but no. Instead, Jack shared his memory of Leeds winning the title at Anfield; a story I had already heard in David Peace's epic 'Shankly' (a holiday-spoiling, reading marathon, that I once foolishly entered).

For those of you unfamiliar with the Anfield story it goes something like this: Liverpool had been top lads under Shankly. However, Leeds were beginning to put together a team that - although boring - could possibly knock Liverpool off their perch. And that is exactly what they did. Culminating in winning the title, at Anfield. You may be thinking that there is nothing particularly heroic in this recitation as yet. However, Martin then shared why it was Jack's most memorable moment and in doing so why Jack was Martin's footballing hero. After Leeds had won the title, Revie told the players to go back out onto the pitch to thank the supporters. At this stage the crestfallen Kop started to sing to the Leeds team: "Champions. Champions. Champions." In my book (much shorter than David Peace's) a heroic gesture, and correctly identified as such.

Martin later told me something even more remarkable regarding the Charltons. He informed me that Bobby and Jack's dad had not watched his sons play in the World Cup final at Wembley. The reason being that he completed his shift down the pit, as otherwise another man would have had to work his shift, which he did not think was fair. Imagine that. Both sons in the World Cup final and you decide to work because otherwise …. Now that's what I call heroic.

Who is your footballing hero and why? If I get enough interesting responses (leeingh@gmail.com) I will publish them.

Chapter 17

Talking with other supporters

As opposition supporters will confirm, I magnanimously believe that my team, is no better nor worse than any others. Except, I expect some form of gratitude from other supporters, as I am a supporter of one of the founder members of the football league; in the country that gave the game to the world. Put succinctly, if we hadn't bothered, your team would not be playing the game today. In philosophical terms, I believe they call this a 'truism'. In my opinion, Burnley FC should receive royalties from other football clubs around the world. Or at least Burnley supporters should be bought a pint by supporters of clubs that were not founding members of the football league.

About five seasons ago, I made one of the best football decisions I have ever made, when I started drinking in Burnley Cricket Club before and after the game. In the last five years, the cricket club has become the designated watering hole for the away support and myself. In case you have not achieved your bucket-list desire to visit Turf Moor, Burnley is unique in that our cricket ground is directly

OURS: FOOTBALL

Headingley LitFest 2020

I WOULDN'T START FROM HERE:
THE SECOND GENERATION IRISH IN BRITAIN

**THURSDAY
5TH MARCH
19:30**

Readings, Q and A, music,
refreshments.

This event is part of our
contribution to LEEDS
LIT FEST 2020

Headingley Community
Hub and Library
North Lane, LS6 3HG

Edited by Ray French, Moy McCrory and Kath McKay, this publication was described by The Irish Times as a 'brilliant, ground-breaking book... Hilarious, heartbreaking diaspora tales'.

'In the old joke, an Irish boomerang doesn't come back, it just sings about coming back' – Ian Duhig, poet. Ray French on his father: 'Our man to man talks went like this. Don't ever get married boy. If you feel lonely, get yourself a dog. Go on now, go out and play'. Meanwhile Kath McKay's mother sat, 'Surrounded by an electric fish, a plastic parrot that played Born Free...and the switch that turned on the electric dog'. Moy McCrory explores what authenticity and belonging mean to a writer, and reflects on a Catholic past with its imagery of saints and miracles.

This collection of fiction, poetry and memoirs is the first book about the second-generation Irish written by the second-generation Irish, rather than an academic or psychological paper about them. It reflects writers torn between two cultures: 'outsiders among the English, we were outsiders among the Irish too'- Ian Duhig.

The evening features **Ian Duhig, Ray French, Moy McCrory** and **Kath McKay,** who all live in Leeds, and who are pictured in that order in a photo by Vincent Burke. The event is organized in collaboration with the Irish Arts Foundation as part of the 2020 Irish History Month.

IrishArts
Foundation

STILL BELONG TO US?

Passionate Burnley fan Lee Ingham (pictured) hopes to get fellow football fans in general onside with his new book about his undying love for the game and its heroes. He writes: 'It is about my team, my dad, my mates. However, it could easily be about you, because the game is ours. The book holds up a mirror to our world of football and asks whether football still belongs to us. If so, what can we do to keep it ours?

FRIDAY
6TH MARCH
19:30

This event is part of our
contribution to **LEEDS**
LIT FEST 2020

New Headingley Club
St Michael's Road LS6 3BG

Free – Pay What You Can

adjacent to the football ground. The stand adjacent to the cricket ground is used by the away support and it too is unique (I believe) in that it had under seat heating! Albeit for one game, as "after the first time it was used, chairman Bob Lord deemed it uneconomical and expensive, and it was never again switched on" (Wikipedia). If you don't believe me then why not check under the seats the next time you are there.

The reason why starting to drink in the cricket club has been one of my best football decision ever, is that I have met people with whom I have a lot in common - we love our club and the game. Prior to this, I had gone in the back room of The Parkview, the pub adjacent to the ground. Away supporters never came into the Park View especially the back room. For good reason. When I think back I have been pretty stupid. As an old friend of mine[21] once said: why are you fighting with the people with whom you have the most in common?

Nowadays, I go out of my way to talk to their supporters and to be friendly with them. I usually ask them about their players and they usually ask me something about our club. We usually end up shaking hands and wishing each other a good game. And the world is a better place for it. Some of you reading this may be thinking: big deal. So what? Others

---

[21] Kathryn Rushton, who not surprisingly is a woman; in case you hadn't tippled it.

will realise how big a deal it is and will realise the error of our ways. However, it is never too late to give it a go, so why not come and join me upstairs at Burnley Cricket Club.

SECTION FOUR

SINGING ABOUT OUR GAME

Boilings drawing of me somehow singing with
Chris Slamon and other Man City supporters?

Many of us would never dream of singing in public. Not even karaoke when drunk. However, we are very willing – in fact keen – to share our love of our game at the top of our voice. In fact, for some of us, we have no choice. It is for this reason that I have never watched Burnley in the opposition's end.

Technically, this section is probably the most difficult aspect of our game to write about. Like taking photographs of the countryside you can never do justice to football chants. In some sense, you really do need to be there. That said I'll give it my best shot. Please familiarise yourself with the tune before joining along.

I will leave it with you to decide whether these are songs or chants.

Chapter 18

Favourite Burnley chants:

Let's start with my favourite chant for players. Winston White was a winger for Burnley in the late 80's and one of our first black players, and we used to sing: 'He's black, he's White, we play him on the right, Winston White, Winston White.'

Although after our play-off victory at Wembley, I did enjoy singing deep into the night, a serenade to another Burnley winger. To the tune of Frankie Valli's 'Can't Take My Eyes Off You': 'der-der-der-der-der, der-der-der-de-der. Der, der, der, der! I love Chris Eagles, you are the love of my life. I love Chris Eagles, you can shag my wife. I love Chris Eagles, I want curly hair too.'

In this song, I love the passion (you can have my life and shag my wife), the humour (I want curly hair too – despite most of us being no-hairs) but mainly I love the crescendo of der,der, der, ders. It's a great band-of-brothers feeling, when thirty or forty of you walk around King Cross, building a crescendo of der-ders, before proclaiming your fondness for one of your promotion-winning players.

A good chant at the expense of your local rivals is an essential for any football supporter. In Burnley's case, our signature tune and most sung in the time I have been watching Burnley, is a song against our rivals; rather than in favour of our club.

'No Nay Never' is a song that I have sung thousands of times despite having reservations about its validity. The chorus, to the tune of I've Been a Wild Rover, is:

No Nay never

No nay never no more

Will we play, Bastard Rovers,

No never,

No more.

My questioning of its validity is rooted in us not playing Rovers for sixteen seasons because they were in a higher league. Consequently, every time we belted it out – which was lots, it reminded me that we were not playing them because they had a better team!

A far better song against our rival was in the 2016 -17 Premier League season when, despite being everyone's favourite to go straight back down to the Championship, we managed to stay up for our first time ever. In the same season, Rovers were relegated from the Championship, a gift from the footballing gods, although as an atheist, I do not believe that the football gods exist. I would buy a pint for whoever wrote this, to the tune of Yellow Submarine:

'Burnley staying up and the Bastards going down,
Bastards going down,
Bastards going down.
'Burnley staying up and the Bastards going down,
Bastards going down,
Bastards going down.'

So far, so good. However, the next bit incorporates a move – all best chants do:
'We're staying up' (you get out of your seat and point to the sky)
'They're going down' (sit down and point to the ground en route)
'We're staying up' (stand up and point)
'They're going down' (sit down and don't forget to point down)

My first sight of 2,500 Clarets doing this as one, in the Cricket Field stand, is one of the funniest things I have ever seen at Turf Moor. And, you'd be surprised how many choruses of this song you can do without getting tired.

Finally, my all-time favourite Burnley chant is currently rarely used and it is an Elvis song. Maybe its demise reflects the eventual demise of the King. It captures what our team mean to us (to the tune of Wise Men Say):
"Take my hand,
take my whole life too,
for I can't help falling in love with you.
The Burnley! The Burnley!"

Least favourite chant and biggest disappointment of a song was the one we used for Glenn Little: 'Super, super Glen. Super, super Glen. Super, super Glen. Super *Glenny* Little'. Glenny! For one of my all-time favourites.

I also did not appreciate the chant levelled at me and other supporters making a late entrance at Turf Moor in the seventies. In those days, the gates opened with twenty minutes to go for people to leave. At this stage, supporters were allowed to join the rest of the throng for free, using an entrance on the Bee-Hole End. There were usually about 100 of us and in my case I was usually coming from my second game of football that Saturday. This was at a time when I was playing for college in the morning and a men's team in the afternoon. Thus stopping me from making Burnley's 3pm kick off. The men's team played in a park near to Turf Moor and so soon as the game finished I ran down to the Turf, declining quick use of the 'shower' facilities (one small sink in the corner of a 'changing room'). As I entered the ground, face normally still soiled with mud from the game I had just finished, we were usually welcomed by the Longside with:
"Part-time supporters, clap-clap-clap-clap-clap
Part–time supporters, clap-clap-clap-clap-clap."

A more endearing Longside song and probably the most surreal chant I have heard goes back to the days when there were still skinheads around. I remember singing – to the tune of – name that tune:
"Doc mart,

cherry red,
juicy bell ender.
Doc Mart,
cherry red,
juicy bell enders."

This celebration of the colour of a pair of boots, worn by a few of the Longside faithful, provides strong evidence for terracing to be reinstated right now. As does another Doc Mart related chant, to the tune of 'Tip Toe Through The Tulips' (yes, they don't write them like that anymore):
"Tip toe, through the Longside,
through the Longside, get your head kicked in
Tip toe through the Longside with me."

And finally, a song that falls into neither the category of away fan nor Burnley fan. It happened at a visit to an Accrington Stanley game, with a group of Burnley supporters, after our game against Chelsea was rescheduled. Stanley were playing Forest Green, the world's only vegan club. Yes, you read it right. The game was at 0 v 0. And we - Burnley supporters on tour – started a chant (to the same tune as Doc Mart cherry red) :
"Meat pie,
Sausage roll,
Come on Stanley score a goal.
Meat pie,
Sausage roll,
Come on Stanley score a goal."

From memory, their manager (a right misery) even stopped scowling and smiled for a moment, before he later asked the stewards to throw us out. Or more specifically, throw Jeff Brown out.

Chapter 19

Favourite 'away' supporter chants

The brevity of this chapter, shows that in at least one sense, the game is still ours. Although I love hearing the away support singing their songs I am probably not on my own in my failure to remember them. But here goes ….

One of my favourites chants I heard was in a south Leeds pub, before a Leeds United game, back in the day when they played Man United. I remember it because of the conceit and bold confidence with which this Man United supporter single- handedly executed this kamikaze chant. If I remember it right it goes:

"We are one of those teams you get now and again
We often score five
And we sometimes score ten

We are the pride of all Europe,
The cocks of the North,
We hate the Scousers,
The Cockneys of course,
And LEEDS ……"

What adds to its quality is the emphasis on Leeds, mimicking the primordial way in which Leeds supporters herald their club. This makes it almost poetic. As if plucked from the Leeds born Tony Harrison's poem 'V'. Where Leeds supporters again get an unfavourable mention. By one of their own.

However, my favourite 'away' chant was sung by Burnley fans (quelle surprise) on behalf of Oxford United. It was before the Longside was knocked down, to be replaced by an all seater poor relation of the Longside. Oxford hadn't brought many and they had made very little noise, so someone must have decided that we would sing a song, literally for them. So we serenaded their scant following - across the no man's land that separated both sets of supporters, with:

'Oxford, Oxford, ra –ra - rah!
Oxford, Oxford, ra –ra -rah!"
'Oxford, Oxford, ra –ra - rah!
Oxford, Oxford, ra –ra -rah!"

What made it special was, that the whole Longside, sang it in a posh voice to strengthen its authenticity.

Bye the way – whatever happened to the phrase 'away from home'; the fuller version of watching your team at a place other than your home ground.

SECTION FIVE

IS FOOTBALL STILL OUR GAME?

Boiling, Bully and me stood with two others, one of whom –
moustache man – looks like he could be one of the better looking
followers of Blackburn Rovers

Increasingly I hear myself say to people like my Dad, that I do not watch / like / enjoy football any longer. Like others, I also hear myself saying that football is 'all about money nowadays' and 'it's not even entertaining'. Recently, I have even thought that I have watched my club 'enough' and that football is no longer the be-all-and-end-all in my life as I wind down my playing 'career' (if only). Then something always stirs, deep down, driven by nature and nurture. And I hear myself saying something like:

'I want my game back!'

This section asks the question - as they say nowadays – is football still 'our game'? In response this section includes a range of witness statements to assist you to draw your own conclusion. You may feel that you already have sufficient evidence to decide whether the game is still ours or not, in which case, just skip to my conclusion, to check whether you are right or not.

Chapter 20

Football is no longer ours

The first witness statement

Today is start of the season Saturday morning. An exciting period in the footballing calendar. The kind of Saturday morning, where you read the football section of the newspaper, whilst eating your breakfast. The kind of Saturday, where you journey to the ground, watch your team, eat a pie (or two), washed down with a couple of pints, to get home in time for MOTD. In other words, the 5-a-Saturday, for football supporters. This balanced diet is restorative for the mental health of the football supporter. Such a day, has been engineered to accommodate the working man, on his (yes that's right) day off. But oh no, not today.

Instead this Saturday will be Football Focus. Then a big gap, between final results and MOTD. Both of which Burnley will not appear in. Instead, it will be a text to my mate, saying that **tomorrow's** kick off is 1.30pm (not 1pm) and that we will be setting off at 11.30 instead of 11.00. And that is it, the sum total, of my footballing Saturday diet.

So what is behind this footballing hate-crime? Why have I had my footballing heritage Saturday stolen from me? The answer is simple. As captured, in my facebook posting, this morning: #skyandpremiershipkilledfootball.

To drum home my point: tomorrow I will be talking to Palace supporters who have had to travel to Burnley and back on a Sunday. I will not be talking to those supporters that decided the journey was not worth undertaking on Sunday. But these people – to whom their club belongs – appear to be less important than other people e.g. those sat in Woodies, with the game on in the background, volume not even on! Or less important than the Woodies landlord, who reluctantly puts the game on, probably thinking as he does: I-hope-Burnley-get-beat-and-Lee-calls-in-on the-way-home-so-that-I-can-take-the-piss-out-of-him[22].

We want our game back. Our Saturdays back. And that's why I do not have and never will have, Sky or BT Sport.

I need to finish here, because I am off out for a late breakfast, to 'Café Lento', with my daughter. Where it gets even worse, as I am beaten at Rugby Union Top Trumps, by my daughter.

---

[22] Somehow Burnley won 1 v 0 and Alan was not in the pub after. Although the manager of Crystal Palace (Frank De Boer) may have retired to the pub. After losing this game, his fourth in charge, he was sacked. More evidence of the madness of the money-fuelled premiership.

And this, is supposed to be start-of–the-season-Saturday? Rugby? Café Lento? Daughter?

The second witness statement

In the 2016 /17 season, Arsenal experienced the 'horror' of not getting in the top four for the first time in 22 years. In the same season, in the same league, Burnley came 16th and our manager was hailed as manager of the season.

Following this heinous crime, Arsenal were in 'civil war' (Ian Wright's words), over whether the manager should be kept. This in the week that Wenger led Arsenal out at Wembley in the FA Cup Final! I promise you I am not making this up.

The sub text to this 'civil war' is 'obviously'[23] money, with Arsenal for the first time missing out on access to Champions League money. The madness of this situation is that one of the biggest criticisms of the beleaguered Arsenal manager is that he does not spend enough money!

It is against this backdrop that the 67% American owner (sic) is offered £1 billion for his shares by a 30% Russian owner (sic again). It is against this backdrop that the American owner (sic

---

[23] I say obviously but to a lot of commentators it is not obvious. They genuinely appear to think, that possibly one of the best managers ever, is now shite!

again) says to the 'stock exchange' (yes - not the supporters but the NY Stock Exchange) that Arsenal "are not, and never have been, for sale"; we will not ask how he came by 'his' 67%. He then goes onto to say that his 'corporate vehicle' (I promise I am still not making this up) is a "committed, long-term investor in Arsenal and will remain so". The backstory to this is that the American, whose shares in six years have risen in value from £12,000 per share to £18,000 per share, thinks that there is more money to be had in 'his' (sic) investment. Consequently, he is not selling to the Russian yet (although he did later, despite it not being for sale). At this stage I would like to remind you that this is a book about football.

The third witness statement

I am on holiday, reading the local paper, wondering whether Strathspey Thistle v Brora (whose cup exploits I have been following since I arrived in Scotland) is taking place at the nearby Grantown-on-Spey?

I am distracted by a half a column piece entitled: 'TV deal drops to £4.4 billion.' The short piece, reports that Sky has maintained its position as the main broadcaster of live Premier League football after agreeing payment for four of the seven packages of television rights, for 2019 -22. The piece states that 'the league's main partner[24] since its inception in 1992', had picked up 128 games, including all

---

[24] In crime

the matches on Fridays, Sundays and Monday evenings. All of which are times when it is difficult for me to get to games. The article ends with a chilling figure; the 'cost-per-game-figure' - to use their jargon. The article reports that for the 2019 -22 seasons, games have been sold for £9.3 million per game, as opposed to the £10.2 million that they are currently being sold for. A further indication of our games financial value was reported in the following day's Scotsman, where it claimed that 'investors' had given a 'thumbs up' to Sky with their share value raising 2 per cent the day after agreeing the £4.2 billion deal.

In some ways, this book should finish right here. In that our game – or at least watching our clubs - is obviously being sold and the consequence is Friday, Sunday and Monday night games. We even know how much it is being sold for - £9.3 million per Premiership game. You could probably even work out the profit for Sky shareholders from the £4.2 billion 'investment'.

Except we will not finish here, because, unlike in the national newspapers[25], these pages can be critical of the Premier League. So here goes and I will stick with the jargon of economics.

---

[25] In a pub discussion I found myself talking to a West Ham supporter who had been a football reporter for national newspapers. The Hammer informed me that the editors would not permit any criticism of the premier league because they feared that they would lose access to its newsfeed.

'Opportunity cost' is a term used by economists to describe the cost of a 'foregone alternative'. Investopedia describes it as 'a benefit that a person could have received but gave up to take another course of action.' For example, the benefit of watching your team at Turf Moor on a Saturday afternoon, is given up to watching it on a Monday night, on TV, at my mate's house. Now Adrian has a nice house and a massive big screen, but at the risk of stating the obvious, the 'opportunity cost' for myself is significant. Namely, the loss of my inalienable rights to watch my team, at my ground, with my eyes and my season ticket, on a non-working day. In footballing terms, it is Season Ticket Holders 0 v 2 Investors in Sky. Notice how I kept it as a home fixture?

BTW – the Highland League Strathspey Thistle (the jags) game was bloody postponed. It is looking like my holiday footy fix will be watching Celtic v Zenit St Petersburg, on TV, in the nearby hotel. At least my son and his pal are off to watch it live. Which is my main reason for watching it on Sky in the nearby hotel; although one of my new hobbies is going in the pub on your own on holiday.

The fourth witness statement

Yesterday afternoon I watched our national game, in a half empty Woodies, on a Sunday afternoon. England beat Lithuania. At the same time Scotland were drawing with Slovenia and saying goodbye to their chances of going to the World Cup in Russia. I could not resist a gentle dig at the handful of Sweaties sat in front of the other screen. BTW this does not constitute bullying as they were winning at the time.

Meanwhile, whilst watching another boring England performance, it started to dawn on me how inconsequential our national game has become. Fair enough, we had already qualified but as I looked around the pub, there were men with their back to the screen. Even the Sweaties were only half watching it and they were welcoming the distraction of my gentle goading. So why is this the case? What has happened?

The answer is straightforward. The Premier League! This break-away movement, with all its marketing and monetary might, has made club games more important (sic) than international matches. This has been the case for some time but the Premier League, the clubs and the players, dare not acknowledge the situation. It first came to my attention when Ferguson quietly started to hold more sway than the England manager. It appeared to be him – a Scotsman – who decided whether Man United's Englishmen were available to play for our country.

Ask yourself the question, why it is easier for Sean Dyche to become national manager than Arsenal manager? A question Dyche has also publicly aired. Also ask yourself, why players like Harry Winks and Daniel Sturridge find it easier to get into the England team than their club team? Then compare this with Italy or Brazil, where the god of Sky does not operate. Ask yourself why Southgate has so few English players to choose from? As evidenced by all three of Burnley's current keepers having played for England. We now witness people playing for England who you not only do not recognise but in fact have rarely heard of! In the Lithuania game it was Harry Maguire (before making himself known in the World Cup) and Aaron Cresswell (who I later learned played for West Ham).

Sky and the Premier League are not only stealing our domestic clubs but also the players for our national teams.

The fifth witness statement

Despite the Premier League / Sky / BT Sport hype, football is probably more boring than it has ever been. Both watching and playing. I say this as someone who is watching a Premier League club that everyone thinks is over-performing. I say this despite having come close to depression as a consequence of not playing football for the last 16 months. Most importantly, I say this as someone who is now publicly agreeing with the football world view of my Dad!

The reason why it is so boring is that it is too fast and too win-orientated. Or, more accurately, the game is now about not-getting-beat; as with defeat comes the possibility of the manager being sacked. Almost gone are the days of players expressing themselves. Instead we have skilful players focussing on working hard, pressing and stopping others from playing. Even my group of five-a-side playing veterans, copy the professionals by 'pressing', 'closing down' and making it difficult for one another. This at a time, when our ageing bodies, has made things naturally difficult. At a time when we don't need any more help to look shit!

Chapter 21

Football is still ours

The first witness statement

Today (Sunday), when I have finished writing about football, I am off to watch my son play football, before I go the pub to watch the 4pm game. Tonight I will watch MOTD 2, mainly to see yesterday's highlights of the Burnley game.

Yesterday (Saturday), I watched Football Focus in the morning before reading the football pages to the sports section. I didn't watch a live game as Burnley are away and on the TV (which I watched at the home of a guy who lives locally, who I got to know as a result of us both being Burnley supporters; we have gone on to buying season tickets alongside one another). Obviously, I saw some of the live 5.15 game, when I made sure that I was in the pub for the final scores. Then home for MOTD followed (in bed) by a YouTube link to a French film that included footage of Burnley Suicide Squad.

The night before (Friday) I go to a book-signing, for a book about football. I attend the book-signing after playing a game of five-a-side football. The lads I attend the book-signing with are people with whom I have played football over the last fifteen years.

Tomorrow night – Monday if you are still following – I am playing five a side, after watching a bit of the FA Cup quarter final (Man Utd v Chelsea) on terrestrial television.

As I say, 'football is everywhere' and 'writing this book has been easy'.

The second witness statement

Andrew Holt is the Accrington Stanley 'owner', or as Holty more accurately explains: "I will never own Accrington Stanley, it belongs to the community and the town. I can't pick it up and take it home, it will never be mine." Andrew Holt 'bought' (sic) the whole club for £1. Now I am not a mathematician but that sounds a lot less than the £1 billion offered by the Russian, for not even the whole-shooting-match, at Arsenal.

They say that a picture tells a thousand stories and for this reason I include a picture of the Chairman of Accrington Stanley (below).

Andrew Holt probably drinking Accy Ale

At the time of writing, Stanley are top of League 2 (4th Division in old money). I went to school with Holty. I used to flick those ears (when they were more prominent) and then scarper before he kicked me with his steel toe-caps. Look at that face. Look, over his pint, into those eyes. Google – Andrew Holt Accrington Stanley. Then listen to him talk. Then ask yourself, 'is the game still ours?' QED.

The third witness statement

It is Boxing Day. We have managed to get two tickets for Burnley's visit to Old Trafford. We are meeting three coaches of Burnley, in a pub in Worsley, to travel to the ground for the 3pm kick off. This is what football should be about.

I am a mix of emotions. I am excited to be watching Burnley at Old Trafford for my first time ever, the excitement added to by my son being by my side for his first ever visit to McTraffords.[26] I am also apprehensive, as four of our back five are not available. However, at half time I am jubilant, as on Boxing Day (first fixture I look for), little old Burnley's second team (not strictly true, as we do not have enough resources to put out a second team), are beating Man United at their 75,000 seater a Theatre of Dreams (although this one was nearly a nightmare as we were winning 0 v 2 – it ended up 2 v 2). At the end we sing to their alleged tourist supporters (to the tune of ai-ai-yipee-yipee-aye), 'it's a long way back to China in a boat, It's a long way back to China in a boat'. I try to start a chant: "we'll be home in an hour, home in an hour".

Before the game, as our coaches pull into Old Trafford's car park, our white bus, with all white passengers, stand out amongst a sea of people who had come from all over the world to take photos of Man United. It is 30 miles from

---

[26] Inside I came across my first ever 'meal-deal' in a football ground. I noticed that each 'vending station' had a controller who was informing his controlees of what was being requested. It tells a story, when a translator is required to interpret someone born in that county. It will come as no surprise that Benedictine was not part of the meal-deal.

Turf Moor to Old Trafford but somehow we stood out like sore thumbs.

"Why are they staring?" asks someone on the coach. "They are not used to seeing so many white faces" suggests another. I look around and there is not one non-white face on the coach. This matches our playing staff who are also white, with the exception of Nahki Wells and someone we've put out on loan. Someone on the bus informs me that L'Equipe had reported this week that Dyche and the club were racist because of the ethnicity of our team.

This is what L'Equipe wrote: "Formed with 80% British players and 100% white players, Burnley is the surprise team of the season. 40 kilo-meters (sic) north of Manchester, everything is from another century. Burnley's team photo is such a programme. Guys with short hair, flattened noses, big ears, ready to fight, who seem to announce their style of play on Saturday afternoon and their lifestyle as Saturday night. There is no single black player in the squad of the 7th-ranked in Premier League, coached by a ginger English-man Sean Dyche (46 years old). And it's as difficult to believe that's premonition as it's coincidence." Maybe it loses something in the translation (premonition?) but surely the authors stereotyping of Burnley's team, hoists him / her with their own petard (a French reference to make any French readers feel at home). I wonder what L'Equipe would make of our mainly white supporters?

So, is Burnley a racist club? Burnley has had its fair share of racists and I knew and still know some of them. But I am very glad to say that the vast majority of racism has now gone. Anyone exhibiting racism nowadays would be thrown out by stewards.

My thinking as to why there are mainly white faces amongst our support is that our club (compared to other Premier League clubs) is followed by men who started attending Burnley matches in the 70's, 80's and early 90's. The other largest group of Burnley supporters are the sons of these men and the coach to the Old Trafford game was made up largely of Dads and the Lads. Consequently, everyone looked like Burnley's supporters in the 70's, 80's and 90's, that is white. I am glad to report that this is beginning to change amongst some of the unaccompanied young Clarets who are other than white.

In my opinion, it is lazy thinking to conclude that our mainly white squad and largely white support, makes the club racist. For instance, I know that the Chairman is not racist (see end notes). Our support has not modified as much as the likes of Man United, with a following that reflects their global marketing efforts. However, I do believe we have a few followers from Yorkshire, as evidenced by probably the most chilling chant that I have ever heard Burnley supporters use : "Yorkshire Clarets we are here, woah, woah. Yorkshire

Clarets we are here, woah, woah.[27]"

The fourth witness statement

Burnley can provide football with another gift (free again), by showing how a club that operates in the biggest league in the world, can still belong to the people that it was set up to entertain. Although the modern game, counter to all the hype, rarely entertains - thanks again Dad.

I remember bumping into Mike Garlick for the first time in about twenty years. In this time, he had gone from being with me on the dole, to becoming Burnley Chairman. Neither of us were on the dole any longer. Upon meeting (prior to an away game) we had an it's-almost-kick-off-time 'elevator talk', in which we hugged, were excited to see each other and he gave me a card from his very big car. In this short reunion, I reminded him that "it is 'our' club, make sure you look after it". I also shared my belief that "it is the club's turn to now look after the town." From what I can see, he has listened to me, and compared to other Premier League club, Burnley has remained 'ours'.

---

[27] I have once attended a meeting of the West Yorkshire Clarets at a pub in the centre of Leeds. Before I sat down, I clarified whether sitting down made me a West Yorkshire Claret, as I was a Burnley Claret and planned to remain so. I am glad that I did sit down as I met some good human beings with who – to put it mildly - I shared interest.

One of the reasons that Burnley FC remains 'our' club is that it still has strong links to the town and its people. For instance, I went to school with Mike Garlick who grew up in Burnley, although I seem to remember ribbing him on the school bus home that he was a Blackpool fan. Another example is that Jimmy McIlroy - our best ever player – although from Northern Ireland settled in Burnley and still lives in the town (see end notes). Finally, many of our sponsors, for instance Oakland Furniture, Farmhouse Biscuits and David Fishwick, are still local businesses and not nationals. In short, many of our supporters were born in the town, although increasingly they may no longer live there[28].

I further illustrate my point that Burnley FC is still ours, by sharing a story written in the first person, a tense used by footballers to help the listener journey into the situation being regaled. The story pays tribute to Jeff Brown, probably the funniest man[29] I know, voice of the Clarets and my brother to another mother.

[28] The causes and impact of people leaving town's like Burnley will be covered in a future book called 'Ours – England'. Inspired by Billy Bragg's book 'The Progressive Patriot'.

[29] For a short while Jeff was a referee in the local league. I remember him telling me about his dream of refereeing Burnley in the FA Cup Final at Wembley and awarding Burnley a corner towards after ninety minutes. Then how as the ball came into the box, he 'rose like a salmon', to head in the winner!

'So it's the 2017 – 2018 Player of the Season award and along with 748 other Clarets I have raised a glass, singing (to the tune of Yellow Submarine) 'the Clarets staying up and the bastards going down, bastards going down, bastards going down. The Clarets staying up and the bastards going down, bastards going down, bastards going down', It is one of those football songs that sometimes captures the zeitgeist – look it up – and gets better the more you sing it.

I am sat on Blakey's table, a lad I went to school with and the manufacturer and donor of Turf Moors 'dugouts' (if they are still called this). Before we get going, we raise a glass to absent friends. Notably Cesc, who I last saw at last years Player of the Season award. The event is compered by someone whose burrrrrrr gives away that he is a little too far down the road for a gig like this; later confirmed as Great Harwood and I would say the Blackburn end of Harwood.

The interloper talks us through the season, introduces the Gaffer, and eventually announces the Players Player of the Year (Michael Keane). Then the Player of the Year Award (Tom Heaton, the best keeper in the league because he gets the most practice) as voted by those at the event. Before the presentation, we have the bit I have been looking forward to the most. A ten-minute presentation from Jeff Brown, the lad I sat with in the 80's on the open ended Beehole End, in the rain, sharing Bovril from his Muppets flask. From memory, I occasionally wore a see through rain hood. Worn, at the time, by my the more mature female i.e. Wolfy had 'borrowed' it off his Mum.

For those of you who do not know BOGOFF (I said buy-one-get-one-free), he has the gift of the gab. He really has kissed the Blarney Stone, which I recently learned is an actual stone in Cork City, which once kissed is supposed to provide the power of speech. Well Jeff must have given it a real good snog. A 'necking', as we used to say. Jeff has become a bit of an after-dinner speaker. He also works for the club doing pre-match and post-match speaking, where his job, basically, is to take the piss out of people. Something he is very good at.

Before the event, after patrolling the marquee to let everyone know that he is amongst us, he comes over to the table. I can see he is a little nervous. And I know why. It isn't public speaking in front of lots of people including the players. He loves that. It isn't that he will not have prepared lines and is therefore at risk of saying the 'wrong' thing. That's his preferred style. It's because, he knows this is his time, to speak on our behalf. About our club. He knows that like the players are privileged to play for our club (as he often tells them), he is also privileged, to speak on behalf of the most important part of our club – us.

If the club provide me with a postscript of what Jeff says I will add it to here

At the end, Jeff leaves the stage and comes and sits back down at our table. 'Hey, Ing what about that?' he asks. I can see from the smile and the twinkle that he is pleased. Despite being drunk, I am also aware of the importance of the first post-match response to his performance. I give him a hug and respond: 'Jeffrey Brown, the voice of the people. Our Club. Our Town' (Town being one of his nomenclatures - a product of Burnley rhyming-slang). Jeff's eyes started to moisten. I begin to feel like Farmer Arthur Hoggett in Babe, after the sheep-pig had won the show, but draw short at saying 'that'll do pig, that'll do'.

The final witness statement:

The final evidence supporting the case for the game still being 'ours' is the Luke Skywalker case, where you just close your eyes and 'feel the force Luke, feel the force.' As they say, 'I must warn you, this involves audience participation'.

For a moment - now is as good as anytime - just stop and ask yourself why, at a time when football is both boring to watch and play, do many of us still have an avid interest in the game? The answer is simple. It is because it actually is 'our' game. It was our fathers, their fathers and our sons. It belongs to our pub friends, the lads we play footy with, the strangers we share football with as an ice breaker. It is part of our DNA.

Going back to my student days, it is an 'a priori truth' that the game is ours. For those of you who did not study Interdisciplinary Human Studies, I mean 'self-evident', for example, all bachelors are unmarried. Or, another example of self-contained evidence, football just is ours. It cannot be taken from us.

Chapter 22

But for how long?

Next time you are watching your club, look around the ground and check how many 'unaccompanied' young people you can see. I bet you it is not many. It would be interesting to know the trend for the age of the people attending games. My hunch is that the crowd is becoming older which is definitely the case around where I sit at Turf Moor. This is probably partly because young people nowadays have a wider range of things to do other than watch football. There also seems to be a growing number of relatively cash and time rich elders who are taking advantage of the good rates offered to seniors.

My own theory is that the increased flight from towns to cities, means that there are probably more people like my son, who supports a team from a place where he has never lived. Consequently, he does not have Burnley mates other than his Dad and his Dad's mates. On reflection, no wonder he only uses his season ticket a few games per season! Is his 'support' sustainable?

In the big picture, I am glad that the game belongs to the world. That is one of football's attractions. However, football is also a way of expressing national and local identity. I know that there can be problems associated with expressing this identity and I tell our kids 'that we are no better and no worse than anyone else'. For instance, very deep down, I do not believe that Burnley people or Lancastrians are better than anyone else. This will come as a surprise to those who know me. However, it goes without saying that we are definitely no worse than anyone else!

Compared to other Premier League Clubs, Burnley FC is still ours, it belongs to people like me born in the town. But for how much longer? For instance, I have heard speak of Chinese owners and who will be the next generation of Clarets? Would someone like my son ever write a book like this? I guess not. Because, sadly, it is not as much his club as it is mine. And before you say, so why doesn't he support Leeds? Well even Leeds supporters are at risk of losing their club.

SECTION SIX

WHAT CAN WE DO?

Our game does not have to go quietly into the night. Here are a few suggestions of things we can do.

Chapter 23

Speak truth to power

If we want to keep this game, we need to keep speaking to one another and those in positions of so called power.

Below is an extract from the Sun (sorry) on 23rd November 2017, where Andrew Holt (you should know who he is by now) shares the ten major changes he wants to see in football, in the 'Stanifesto' (the Sun does have good headlines though):

"10. Thou shalt not speak - no more, I say!
Very few owners and chairmen are prepared to publicly say what they really think about the football set-up. This is a real problem for the future of the game. Football authorities actually threaten funding if owners speak out. The rich clubs in the Prem run the game. They decide the agenda on academies, transfer windows, funding, TV money and the rest. The EFL has no option but to go along with them because they are the paymasters. Fans know this and continually tell

me this. They are not stupid - they feel the EFL and its clubs bow to every whim of the top flight. Their feelings are not without merit. And if we do not want another situation where fans are boycotting their own clubs as in the Checkatrade Trophy, we had better start listening to them and giving them a voice."

To put the 10th point of the Stanifesto in context, on 10 May 2017, the BBC reported that Andrew Holt – in response to news that Pogba's agent received £40 million from him signing for Man Utd – went public and said that Football League clubs were like 'a starving peasant begging for scraps' from the top flight. They also reported that he had tweeted: "Hang your heads in shame, @premierleague you're an absolute disgrace to English football."

The Premier League responded: "We will be writing to Mr Holt to ask him if he wishes the Premier League to continue the support we currently provide for his and other clubs in the EFL."

Holty's response: "What they're saying is not only are they not bothered about it, anybody who complains about it, we'll take your money away and shut you down."

He goes on to say, "Whoever put that out would've been sacked if they worked for me. It was a crazy thing to do. My comments about the agent would've died a death had they not made those threats. We turn over £2m and haven't got a pot to p*** in. You can't have the Premier League bullying the smallest club of the 92, can you?

This is how a club should be. I went to an end-of-season awards at Manchester United once. The players were on a table surrounded by security and my little lad couldn't go near them. What's that? Get me out of here."

Holt has recently discussed his issues with EFL chief executive Shaun Harvey. 'They are definitely listening,' is the message from Accrington's chairman. I hope for everyone's sake that that they are listening. For as Holty states: "There's got to be a better balance of rules and finance to make life more liveable. I'm going to fight tooth and nail to make this club sustainable. Anyone in front of that is going to have to move over, because there's no way I'm letting it go."

Chapter 24

Don't buy football from Sky or BT Sport

Our game is increasingly being changed to accommodate such as the shareholders in Sky and the Qatari's selling TV rights to EFL games in Africa. An obvious example is the change to the time when games are played. From the supporter's perspective, travelling and watching games on Sunday morning or Monday evening does not suit. However, it does suit the people selling the game to TV companies. The irony is that one of their selling points is the presence of supporters at our games! A long while ago, I predicted that we would be paid to be 'extras' in the crowd, at a game played in the early hours of the morning to accommodate the Chinese or Indian market [30]. I still believe this will happen.

It would be interesting to know the rationale behind the Premier League's decision to cap the price of away tickets. Was it in response to calls from supporters and the boycott

---

[30] I once spoke with a Real Malaga supporter who informed that team regularly kicked off at 10pm during the week to accommodate the television. Imagine setting off back from Portsmouth, Plymouth or Exeter after midnight on a school night.

of away games at places like Chelsea and Arsenal? Or was it driven by marketing considerations and recognition that the Premiership is less marketable if the away support is absent?

Chapter 25

Support the
Football Supporters Federation (FSF)[31]

After the Hillsborough disaster, football authorities naturally acted to stop a repeat. But many football supporters would like to stand and it is definitely possible to accommodate this whilst still having a safe stadium. In my opinion, we need to stop treating fans like we are still in the hooligan age. We have to move away from overzealous regulations that can spoil the match-day experience.

For this reason, I have started to support the Football Supporters Federation (FSF). Below is an extract from an email trail that I have been involved in:

---

[31] For every book sold £1 will be donated to the Football Supporters' Federation, which represents football supporters in England and Wales. It campaigns across a range of issues and supports fan representation on clubs' boards, lower ticket prices, and the introduction of safe standing areas at grounds in the top two tiers of English football.

Hi John

I am keen on the authorities considering those who watch games live when scheduling games for those who watch the TV. I am also interested in the reintroduction of safe standing. These are two things that the FSA are trying to move forward and I wondered whether West Yorkshire Clarets would support them in this by - in the first instance - becoming affiliated. Is this something that you have talked to others about already?

Regards

Lee

Hi Lee,

Thanks for your email. You referenced the FSA, which I understand to be the FSF (Football Supporters Federation). West Yorkshire Clarets would not be allowed to affiliate because we are not a structured group with a constitution. However, West Yorkshire Clarets are members of Burnley FC Supporters Groups (mentioned in previous email) at which we are represented by one member of our mailing list at monthly meetings at Turf Moor. As a consequence, the Burnley FC Supporters Groups ARE already affiliated to the FSF.

The Burnley FC Supporters Groups are also members of the FSF's Premier League Fans Group and in this instance, are represented by Tony

Scholes (uptheClarets.com). Among the topics discussed, which are taken to the Premier League by that group, include both of the ideas you mentioned (TV and safe-standing) - each very much on the current agenda.

So, in short, WYC are members of BFCSG, who in turn are affiliated to the FSF and are actively involved. I hope that makes sense.

Best wishes

John Robertson, WYClarets

It makes sense now John. Although, your response did make me think that I had mistakenly asked him: 'are you the Judeans People's Front?'

On the back of this I requested support from the three MP's who I know personally - John Grogan MP for Keighley used to be our five-a-side goalie and two others through work, plus Julie Cooper MP for Burnley (see end notes) In my letters I outlined my concerns and referred to the safe seating trial that had taken place in Scotland. From all four I received a positive response. However, my response from our representative on the FSF's Premier League Fans Group was less positive: "We've been working with Burnley's MP and the other local MPs for some time on this. The debate won't get anything like the Longside we remember though, there is no likelihood at all of a return to terracing." Tony Scholes may be right. But surely it's worth a try and maybe the first step – literally – in the right direction.

Chapter 26

Nationalise the game

What's happening to our game – at least the Premier League - is analogous with what Thatcher did with our water supply. To remind you, the water industry was privatised in 1989, transferring the assets and personnel of the 10 water authorities into limited companies.

Listen to John McDonnell's explanation of water privatisation and tell me what you think. Citing figures from the National Audit Office, the Shadow Chancellor told the *Observer,* that water bills had risen by 40% in real terms since privatisation of the industry in 1989. In 2017, privatised water companies paid out a total £1.6bn to their shareholders. Since 2010, the total was £13.5bn (The Guardian, 17 Feb 2018). For our water! Isn't privatisation effectively what has happened to the Premier League? Aren't football clubs also floated on the stock market and also owned by large foreign shareholders?

So what can we do? Well, we could take a leaf out of Jeremy Corbyn's book. Speaking at a conference on alternative models of ownership, Corbyn stated:

"The next Labour government will call an end to the privatisation of our public sector, and call time on the water companies, who have a stranglehold over working households. Instead, Labour will replace this dysfunctional system with a network of regional, publicly owned water companies. We can put Britain at the forefront of the wave of change across the world in favour of public, democratic ownership and control of our services and utilities." He goes onto to say that we need to be "at least as radical" as the 1945 Labour government that created the National Health Service (The Guardian, 17 Feb 2018).

Am I alone in thinking that our national game is one of our national 'services and utilities'? Am I alone in wanting our government to be radical and to start working for the people to which football really belongs? Am I alone in thinking, 'for the many, not the few'? I hope I am not alone. Feel free to join me in saying, it is 'ours'. Give us it back. And while we are at it, let's do the same for water, electricity, gas and the railways.

Chapter 27

Stanleyise the game

And all of our clubs

Accrington were one of the 12 founders of the football league. Sandwiched between Burnley and Blackburn, in the 2017/18 season they had the second smallest attendance (1,979) of the 92 league teams. With a turnover of £2 million per annum. However, or because of this, "Accrington is like a time capsule. It's what football has lost" according to their Chairman, Andy Holt.

At my first ever visit to their ground I received a flavour of what football had lost and I can safely say that Accrington Stanley v Forest Green is the one of the best footballing days I have ever had; helped by the Burnley supporters with who I attended (Burnley v Chelsea had been cancelled). From the taxi driver (an Asian guy who sang us a Stanley song) to the Chairman, everyone was approachable, friendly and passionate about 'their' club. The club takes pride in it belonging to the supporters and town. For instance, the Chairman explained to me that the manager's and players' work does not finish when the whistle blows for 90 minutes. They are told that they all need to join the rest of the club, in the clubhouse, after the game.

Amongst 'the rest of the club' I spoke to one guy who had rattled collecting tins at Burnley and Blackburn games when Accy were struggling financially (Burnley were more generous and let them in for free). Now that's what I call support.

I also met a group of Norwegian supporters who were on their annual pilgrimage to Stanley and they had sponsored the game (£400). I asked them how they came to support Stanley and they explained that they had met some girls in Barcelona fifteen years ago and that the girls told them they were from Accrington. So they looked up the place and discovered that the town had a football league team. Consequently they have visited the ground once a year for the last fifteen years.[32] By the of the evening they had the whole club – including the Chairman, players and Manager - singing a Norwegian Stanley chant. That's right. Everyone – including players – singing a Norwegian Stanley chant: "Lo-lo-delo delo-delo-lo-delo STANLEY" feel free to join in. In case you didn't know, it is inspired by Norway's 1980 entry into the Eurovision song contest. You'll be glad to hear that it is available on YouTube.

The bonviviality (proper word) was helped by the fact that Stanley had won and had remained top of the fourth division. I ended up drinking with Stanley's Manager (John Coleman) tapping his knowledge about whether Wigan's Paul Cook (and former Stanley Manager) would make a good Burnley Manager (he would). I also spoke with Stanley's playmaker (Jordan Clarke) who I had earlier watched beat four men to score candidate for goal of the season. I ended the evening on the centre circle, with the Chairman, in my John Motson coat, whilst it was snowing, singing Stanley songs. BTW – it was £10 admission and there is a happy hour of £1 a pint after the game if Stanley win!

Andy Holt is right when he says: 'this is how a football club should be'. However, I hope he is wrong when he refers to the

---

[32] Even more bizarre was their response to my next question: 'And what about the girls?' To which they replied: 'We've never met them. We don't think they even came from Accrington.' And, now here's a line: 'We did not find the girls but we found a football team.'

club being in the footballing past. Because I hope that it's 'the future' and that other clubs learn from Accrington Stanley and start operating like them. It is a club for supporters, by supporters. A club that is aware of its purpose. As the Great Man says, "The future for Stanley is as a supporters club, there is no other option and success depends on how much we integrate the club back into the community." And, "Doesn't matter what league we're in, it's a day out, the best day out in football when I've finished." Holty and Stanley's mission may be driven by the club having relatively little financial resource but just imagine what you could do with more finances? If you were so inclined.

Accrington Stanley are not alone. Our game has been found again by clubs like the 'recently' formed FC United or the reclaimed Portsmouth (sadly resold to private ownership). If they won't play ball (the football variety) then why not take our ball back?

At the back of Accrington Stanley's achievements is a simple but important value, captured in yet more wise words from Andrew Holt: "Remember the club belongs to the town and its townsfolk." The key words here are 'the club'. Football clubs were formed by local people for the common advantage of local people. When I think 'club' I think of membership and ownership. Andrew Holt recognises and adheres to their full title i.e. Accrington Stanley Football **Club**. If more clubs adhere to their full title, then the game would remain, 'ours.'

Chapter 28

Not an option –

Why not start supporting another club? Whilst writing this book I had a sad pre-match conversation with a passionate Southampton supporter. Bedecked in his team's colours, he informed me that he was not renewing his season ticket, as he is "sick of the Premier League". Instead, he is going to "watch a local non-league team" that will cost him "about £10 for a game, pie and a pint" and it "will not involve all the bullshit that is involved with football nowadays. I am sick of it!" He did not speak in anger. He spoke reservedly, regretfully and with a conviction that he was actually going to do it. This was confirmed by his girlfriend, who was also bedecked in Southampton plumage. She assured me that he really would be giving up Southampton Football Club at the end of the season.

As I listened to him I could have cried. Yet I wanted to hug him, which is something I have never done with an unknown away supporter, unlike many a Burnley supporter, after we have scored. In the Southampton supporter I saw myself and other supporters. His passion and love of the game was sufficient that it hurt him to see it being stolen from him. His club had been taken from him. The hurt was enough that he was going to give up the very thing that he loves.

In writing this, I started to think that maybe the Southampton guy is right and that another club may return football to him. And then I started to think the unthinkable, could I give up my club and firm up my association with a club like Guiseley FC? I am off for a 14 mile run to think the unthinkable[33].

---

[33] However, as a pub pal once informed me, football clubs are like your Mum and Dad. Just because you know they're better ones, you're not going to change them. As I said, 'the unthinkable'

CONCLUSION

APNA

I know that there is nothing as certain as change. However, hopefully the book has shown that 'football' still remains 'ours'.

Define 'ours' I hear you say. Well seeing you asked, for me it means 'belonging to us'. Define 'us'? My definition of 'us' is the people that play, watch, talk and sing about football.

However, football 'clubs' are decreasingly 'ours', in that, they decreasingly belong to 'us', the supporters of our clubs. Instead clubs increasingly belong to everybody, including sheikhs, shareholders, Sky / BT subscribers and those customers who pay to watch the occasional game and leave before the end if they are not happy with what they have bought. For me, this is sad.

My fear is, that in making football clubs available to everybody, it will kill the game for those who watch their club at football grounds. I hope my book has shown that this is a legitimate fear but also that there is something that we can do to prevent this, or at least slow down the theft of our clubs.

Finally, I recently learned that 'Apna' is a word used in many languages across South Asia meaning 'ours, yours or everybody's'. My hope is, that there is a way, for football to be 'ours, yours and everybody's'. Or, in other words, an Apna FC

EPILOGUE

"HELLO, HELLO, LEE INGHAM IS BACK, LEE INGHAM IS BACK"

I had planned to stop writing this book once I started playing again. However, this part of the book was written the evening after I played my first game in 16 months. Litterally, I could not stop myself.

To add authenticity, it is written in footballer-speak (a dying art) making a mazy run between the past and present tense, first person and whatever the other option is: So there I am in the goals, getting a feel for the game that I'd missed so much, completing the finishing stretches for what has to be the world's most stretched hamstrings. I shout, "next keeper", thus inviting someone to replace me in goals. So out I come, after sixteen months of footballing abstinence. I automatically adopt my go-to position at the centre of defence. At first, I miss a few passes, tackles, kicks. But I also complete a few. Then my chance comes, to express myself, with a Joe Jordanesque - England v Scotland – dummy. Scouse Neil completely buys it. Even better he goes public and admits that he can't believe he's fallen for it. Other players remind him of how much he had bought it. I smile. Lee Ingham is back!

After the game, we retired to the pub. Despite people having not seen each other for a long time, the talk was almost singularly, about football. As per usual, my awareness heightened by my sixteen-month absence, the discussion was mainly about how shit football has become. Plus, some post match analysis of the game we had just played in. Obviously, the analysis includes jibes at each other expense. Mainly mine. Then Scouse Neil introduces a new kid to the block in sharing that he had paid £100 for an ice-bath. A new example of the levels we go to continue playing. The general consensus was that it had been a good game.

When I get home, I post on Facebook the return of Lee Ingham. Self-deprecatingly announcing 'the return of a slightly more mature Emlyn Hughes.' Remember, I had grown up hearing my Dad liken me to Hughes, who he called 'the carthorse' (his adaptation of Hughes' nomenclature of 'crazy horse'). Did I say 'self'-deprecating?

APPENDICES

I have placed this anecdote outside of the main body of 'Ours' for reasons that will soon become apparent.

This appendix is to remind us that some people do not live in the world of football. I 'include' it, to counterpose the rest of the book. For those who do not inhabit planet football, this next bit may come across as a no –ry [34] i.e. not a story. But for those that reside on planet football, here goes:

Talking to a lad in the pub, ask him:

"Did you play Monday?"

"No, I've stopped playing" (context: at this stage I had not played for six months and would have killed to play).

"Ok, why's that?" I enquire.

"Well I've been busy at work and I've realised that the more I play the worse I get" (context: the latter has never stopped me).

"What do you mean?" Me still showing an interest.

"Well I only started playing 6 months ago."

"How old are you?" Increasingly bemused.

---

[34] Thank you Ste Kane for this phrase. BTW it is not coincidental that you also appear in the appendices to the football section of the book.

"**Forty-two.** I played a Lads and Dads game and thought I'll give it a go and enjoyed it at first. It was a good work out."

"So, let's get this right. You are forty-two and you've just started playing!"

"Yeh."

"Who's your favourite player?"

"I have not got one."

"Who's your team?"

"Not got one. I got free tickets last season to watch some Leeds games but stopped going because the team were negative and everyone sat around me was negative. I started going the bar at half time and not going back out. Then I stopped going."

"Really?" as in 'this cannot be real'.

Mouth wide open, I go to make water at the toilet.

On return he informs me: "Yes I started playing 6 months ago and I retired three months ago."

I have not made the above up. It is all true[35].

---

[35] When I shared this story with another non-footballing friend he took umbrage and asked how come he wasn't getting a mention in the book? My response was that if I ever write a book about getting regularly put to the sword at racquetball by myself then he would get plenty of mentions. Is that enough of a mention Nigel Oddy?

END NOTES

Centre half - I have had to give up the enforcing aspect of this position, as I cannot even kick people as well as I used to. Although, according to Pete McCarthy, I committed one of the dirtiest fouls he has ever seen. It was in the final of a 5-a-side cup and it was against a centre forward who from memory played for Norway women's team. As customary, early in the game, I let the forward know that I was there but because she was so slight she fell to the ground very easily. To a chorus of boos from the lads watching. In my defence it was the final and I didn't want to patronise her. After all, it's a man's game. Even if you are a woman!

Clothes - This is also true of my clothes the most of which I have been given by a similar-sized friend or secured from the weekly yard sale at the local hospice . Where incidentally I also secured the mother of our kids. The exception to the second-hand rule is socks and undies. Although, I once bought two pairs of second-hand undies from a jumble sale (rules are for breaking) and gave one pair to my Dad as a Christmas present. For a while, we had matching undies, XXL yellow plaid. A bit like Burnley's yellow away kit at the time. I am not claiming that the Clarets copied the Ingham's away kit.

Worldwide - You read it right! 'Worldwide'. He has watched every Leeds United game – including friendlies – since 1981. At the time of writing that it the last 2,246 games. He does not include reserve games, which he also watches. I once asked my mate Steve Taylor to quiz Mick and he did so by referring to a business trip to Malaysia in the 90's where Steve had discovered that he was staying at the same hotel as the Leeds United team, who were on a pre-season tour. Mick told him the name of the hotel! When I heard Mick drop the word "worldwide" I felt Mick display the full majesty of his peacock tail feathers. BTW – next time you are with a Leeds United supporter try and encourage them to readopt the title of The Peacocks. I hope you have more success than me. For some reason they seem reluctant.

Mike Garlick - It's the early 90's and we are sat in the lower section of the Longside. In front of us a black opposition player is being berated when he takes throw-ins by a nasty looking group of short-haired men, sat above us on the balcony of one of the corporate boxes. These racist pigs start baying racist comments. At this stage, a man bravely stood up to this group of racists and regaled a loud Churchillian rebuke of their intelligence (lack of it) and humanity (lack of it). His eloquence and bravery was astonishing. I wish I could remember what he said. More importantly, I regret not supporting his stance, unlike the man sat next to him – Mike Garlick.

Jimmy McIlroy - According to my Dad – who recently shook McIllroy's hand and told him that he was his 'all-time hero'. If you are wondering who he is then I share with you my Dad's view that if he'd have played for England (and not Northern Ireland) he would have been a household name. Tommy Finney (who played at the same time) said that McIlroy was the best at the time. McIlroy played for Burnley at a time when they won the First Division. However, he still worked at Burnley colliery and drank in Burnley Miners (the place they sell the most Benedicitine in the world). When Bob Lord sold him to Stoke City, allegedly thousands of Clarets said that they'd not go on Turf Moor again and were true to their word. The former Bee hole End is now named after him. In Mcilroy's days the game belonged to 'us' even more. Not only did 'we' play the game, but 'one of us' was the best player and had part of our stadium named after him. Whilst I was writing this book Jimmy Mcilroy MBE sadly died. Mcilroy, who elected to receive his MBE medal at Turf Moor, was given a good send-off at Turf Moor. As the funeral cortege passed Turf Moor a banner read 'Heroes are remembered but legends never die'. For me the highest accolade is the one I have often heard said by people who were fortunate enough to meet Mcilroy. It is an accolade that recognises his footballing prowess but also transcends football. It is, that he was not just a great footballer but that also, you could never meet a better man. As I said, 'ours'.

Letter to Burnley's MP:

Dear Julie Cooper MP,

I am writing to request your support for Safe Standing at football grounds.

I have regularly attended football games for the last 40 years. In my opinion the removal of the option to stand has been the worst thing to happen to our game. It has helped kill our culture and it is not even safe.

You may be aware of the safe standing that has been trialled at Celtic Football Club. This has gone well and we would like to see it extended to football grounds like my second home (Turf Moor).

I am glad to see that our Labour Party supports safe standing at football grounds. Please support this request

Regards,

Lee Ingham

Dear Mr Ingham,

Thank you for your email. Your view on this is really useful ahead of Monday's debate. I spent many hours as a child with my Dad on the terraces at Turf Moor. Nowadays though I appreciate a seat but I understand that others may prefer to stand and with safe provision, I would support their right to be able to do so. Establishing a Safe Standing area would also have a significant on the price of match day tickets and would put Premier football within the financial reach of more people. Anything which opens football up further is something I am in favour of, as a life-long Burnley fan and a season ticket holder, I understand just how much football gives to this town. I am pleased to inform you I will be supporting this motion, today I will attend the debate on this matter, I also intend to speak at this debate in support of safe standing.

Thank you for sharing your views with me, I will bear them in mind this afternoon.

Kind regards,

Julie Cooper MP

PHOTO GALLERY

Best ever Burnley shirt and best ever player not to play for BFC.
Please ignore the Leeds shorts and socks.
Thanks to Mr Kay for the photo

Under 13's Barden School Second Team. Six of the back row went onto Burnley Grammar School, with four of us playing in the Upper Sixth Second XI (see below). Spot Jeff Brown and myself

Under 14's Burnley Grammar School 1st team photo pre Aidy Hurst days. When we had a proper team. Guess which one is me? Clue – stood far away from Stevie Cool

SECOND XI FOOTBALL

The Second XI this season was older than it has been in recent years, with a large number of players coming from the Upper Sixth. This seemed to be the result of fifth form games being on a Thursday; which meant they couldn't play the Wednesday fixtures. Owing to this change, and because some boys left school to get jobs, the team for the opening months of the season was unsettled. Eventually 36 different players were used throughout the season.

There were a number of memorable games. On the opening day of the season the team beat Q.E.G.S. 3 - 0. The best performance of the opening period of the season was a 2 - 1 win, at Manchester Grammar School, with the opening goal coming from a free-kick by Lee 'Zico' Ingham.

In March came our best overall performance, against Oulder Hill, Rochdale. We beat them 2 - 1 in an exciting game against the best team we played. For the fixture against Bury G.S. we only had ten players, so Carl Denson, who was substitute for the under 16's 'B' team played and scored two goals. This game was followed by our largest win of the season, 13 - 1 over Haywood Sixth Form, Bolton, with Steve Brunton scoring 5 and Simon Raine scoring 4 in his only game of the season.

The top scorers were Steve Brunton 14 and Warrick Ingham 10 in only 14 games. Other players who deserve a mention are Nick Harris (for the most games played); Barry Naylor (for consistency); and Alan Holden (for the most improved player).

On behalf of all those who have played for the Second XI this season, I would like to thank Mr.Grayson for his time on Wednesdays and Saturdays and Messrs.Smith and Sheridan for their time at training (this comes especially from Steve Brunton).

RESULTS:

	P	W	D	L	F	A
	28	14	3	11	67	65

PLAYER	App	Goals	PLAYER	App	Goals	PLAYER	App	Goals
N.Harris	26	1	Sa.Choudhry	21	-	H.Lingard	2	-
L.Ingham	25	5	C.D.Howarth	12	2	S.Emmett	2	-
J.Holland	23	1	L.Jones	9	7	D.Mercer	2	1
B.Naylor	23	1	T.Green	7	1	D.Horner	1	-
G.Moorhouse	19	3	D.Hunt	4	-	C.Denson	1	2
J.Dewhurst	18	-	Al.Blackburn	3	-	S.Raine	1	4
I.Gregory	16	1	A.Cooper	4	-	M.Townend	1	1
A.Holden	18	4	K.Patton	3	1	An.Blackburn	1	-
W.Ingham	14	10	Sd.Choudhry	3	-	T.Knight	1	-
M.Smith	14	5	J.Bushell	2	-	D.Gill	1	-
S.Brunton	13	14	D.Collinge	2	-	J.Phillips	1(+1)	-
W.Symmons	12	1	A.Seddon	2	-	G.Kenyon	2(+1)	-

John Dewhurst. Captain. U6

My daughter's first ever game. At half-time, she said: "Dad, you've sworn 19 times."

First ever match watching with an opposition supporter. Burnley 2 v Everton 1. His is the look of a football supporter, in the away end, after you've thrown away the opening goal advantage. Bye the way, I never knew Chewbaka was a Claret

My Dad and son watching the Clarets on the Longside – the eyes show their passion, or lack of it

A picture of Chris Salmon's favourite player, with the red hair that they shared, despite Chris's denial. Undeniable, is that both Chris and Rodney were many people's favourite.

Blank page to be used to start your own book!
If I can, you can.

Lightning Source UK Ltd.
Milton Keynes UK
UKHW020946270819
348413UK00004B/18/P